GETTING
A PAY RISE

GETTING

A PAY RISE

**Patricia Scudamore and
Hilton Catt**

TEACH YOURSELF BOOKS

For UK order queries: please contact Bookpoint Ltd, 78 Milton Park, Abingdon, Oxon OX14 4TD. Telephone: (44) 01235 400414, Fax: (44) 01235 400454. Lines are open from 9.00–6.00, Monday to Saturday, with a 24 hour message answering service. Email address: orders@bookpoint.co.uk

For USA & Canada order queries: please contact NTC/Contemporary Publishing, 4255 West Touhy Avenue, Lincolnwood, Illinois 60646–1975, USA. Telephone: (847) 679 5500, Fax: (847) 679 2494.

Long renowned as the authoritative source for self-guided learning – with more than 40 million copies sold worldwide – the *Teach Yourself* series includes over 200 titles in the fields of languages, crafts, hobbies, business and education.

British Library Cataloguing in Publication Data
A catalogue record for this title is available from The British Library.

Library of Congress Catalog Card Number: On file

First published in UK 2000 by Hodder Headline Plc, 338 Euston Road, London, NW1 3BH.

First published in US 2000 by NTC/Contemporary Publishing, 4255 West Touhy Avenue, Lincolnwood (Chicago), Illinois 60646–1975 USA.

Typeset by Transet Limited, Coventry, England.
Printed in Great Britain for Hodder & Stoughton Educational, a division of Hodder Headline Plc, 338 Euston Road, London NW1 3BH by Cox & Wyman Ltd, Reading, Berkshire.

Impression number   10 9 8 7 6 5 4 3 2 1
Year   2005 2004 2003 2002 2001 2000

CONTENTS

INTRODUCTION

Most of us feel we're not paid enough for our input as employees or for our various talents. But what happens when we decide to go after better deals for ourselves? What alternative paths are open to us and, in these situations, what works and what doesn't?

There is a commonly held view that getting a pay rise over and above the standard rate is a lot harder than it ever used to be. Why should this be so? Here are a few of the reasons people frequently put forward:

- Flatter corporate structures – a lot of companies have adopted structures that make it more difficult for anyone aspiring upwards pay-wise.
- The fragmented nature of many large companies – the tendency for such companies to be broken down into small, autonomous units and the consequent effect this has on people's pay prospects.
- The growing number of people who work in small firms – opportunities for pay advancement may be limited or simply not available.
- The tendency for companies to be more hard nosed with people and to put up the shutters to those who attempt to negotiate better deals for themselves – the down-grading of people in the ranking of factors that determine the success of businesses.
- The decline of collective bargaining (union muscle) – this is partly because of the steps employers have taken to minimize union influence and partly because of the absence of union representation in the small firm sector where an increasing number of jobs are based.

For a lot of people, therefore, collective bargaining is not available as a means of redressing pay grievances.

■ The fact that many employers are genuinely unable to shell out the cash for large pay increases – this is a fact largely determined by our recent recession-plagued past and the difficulty of maintaining decent profit margins in the face of spiralling and often global competition.

■ A less paternal attitude towards people – the increasingly prevalent view is that it's up to people to look after themselves.

■ The growing number of people who work at home – for these people negotiating a pay increase has intrinsic difficulties.

The bottom line here is another commonly-held view: that the only way to get a decent pay increase is to move on – to go out into the job market and find someone who is prepared to pay you a figure more in line with the talents you can offer.

Whilst changing employers from time to time is something we probably all need to do to advance our careers in the directions we want them to go in, it is nevertheless an activity that carries quite definite risks. Irrespective of how well we research prospective employers, a new job is still largely a step into the unknown. It may turn out to be a good move (it usually does) or it could prove to be a complete and unmitigated disaster – most of us have had experience of both. The point here, though, is that changing employers is not something we want to be doing all the time – and certainly not every time we feel the urge for better pay. We'd be taking more risks than we need to just to achieve a pay rise.

Getting a pay rise is a serious business and it should always be viewed as such. For this reason you will find no quick fixes or golden methods with 'guaranteed' results in this book. In our opinion, quick fixes and golden methods only serve to trivialize the issues and could, in some circumstances, get you into very serious trouble indeed. If there are recipes for success, the ingredients are dogged determination, the application of a little clever know-how and a proper awareness of the risks.

The book is divided into ten chapters – each chapter examining a different way of dealing with a pay problem – whilst the book as a whole provides a structured approach to the issue of pay (where to begin, what to try next and so on). This approach is summarized in the form of a model at the end of the book.

As you work your way through you will come across a number of case studies that will enable you to draw on the experiences of others and learn from their successes and mistakes. At the end of each chapter you will find a section of questions and answers dealing with some of the knottier problems people come across, together with a summary and a verdict on the good points and bad points of the particular approach under discussion (a quick index of what you need to take into account).

When looking for pay rises one fact is certain – to go on year after year feeling under-paid and under-valued will do you no good at all. Sooner or later your confidence and self-esteem will start to sap. Even worse, you may find yourself becoming bitter and envious of others. In short, going after the salary you think you deserve is a task you must never shrink back from. In this respect alone, we hope our book will be helpful reading to you.

1 | BARGAINING

On the face of it, the most direct route to getting a pay rise is by simply going along and asking for one. But what issues do you need to think through first and, when it comes to approaching your boss, what should you be saying? In this first chapter we will look at how to go about making a convincing case for yourself and the circumstances in which it will work. The topics we cover are:

- Rating your chances of success – knowing when what you're asking for may be difficult or impossible to achieve; knowing when all you'll be doing is banging your head on a brick wall
- Sizing up your bargaining power – identifying the factors that are going to lend weight to your case
- Using bargaining postures that invite positive responses
- Handling meetings to discuss pay issues
- Gauging the reaction – what to do when the outcome was not the one you hoped for
- Taking stock and planning your next move
- The importance of credibility

What are your chances?

Before you plunge into negotiations with your employer on an issue such as pay, an important question to put to yourself is 'What are my chances of success?' Why is this question important? For the simple reason that, if you see your chances of success as nil or minimal, going to all the effort of putting up a case probably isn't worth it. Furthermore, being rejected out of hand has a demoralizing effect and this is something you need to avoid.

So what are the factors that are going to influence your chances of success? When you think about it, there are two:

> 1 your employer's ability to pay you the increase you're asking for
>
> 2 whether your employer thinks you're worth it or not.

Let's now look at each of these two factors in a bit more detail.

Your employer's ability to pay

The exercise we're about to embark on is known as **profiling**. Profiling is how you determine your employer's ability to deliver and, in this instance, how you determine your employer's ability to deliver the pay increase you think you deserve. The question you're asking yourself, therefore, is can these people stretch themselves that far or is it going to give them a problem? Here is a checklist that will help you draw up a profile of your employer's ability to pay.

Culture

■ How does your employer score when it comes to handing out pay increases?

■ Are they keen to see that people are rewarded correctly or do they have the reputation of being tight-fisted?

■ How do they view people generally?

■ Do they see people as the key element in the success of the business or do they view them as unimportant and disposable?

Profitability

■ How is your employer's business performing at the moment?

■ Is it profitable?

■ Does it have the resources at its disposal to give out pay increases to people?

■ Is there any trading factor that could have a bearing on the amount of money available (e.g. poor cashflow)?

Differentials

- In giving you the rise that you want, will your employer be inviting problems in other quarters?
- What will your peers think if they should get to know?
- Will they think that they should be afforded the same treatment?

Salary structures

- Is there a fixed scale or salary band for the job function you perform?
- Will the rise you're after put you through the ceiling of the scale or band?
- What flexibility is there to allow this to happen?

Please don't view this checklist as exhaustive. Other factors can also have a bearing on an employer's ability to give pay increases. For example, a company in the throes of a hostile take-over bid may be in no mood for awarding rises. Similarly, a company which is up for sale may have its salaries on ice as part of an undertaking to prospective buyers.

Evaluating the results of profiling

The idea of profiling, remember, is to get you to give some proper thought to rating your chances of success with your bid for more pay. One of the main purposes of the exercise is to halt you in your tracks if you rate your chances as nil or poor. Your company has just announced record losses; a freeze on salaries has recently been imposed by head office; the rise you're looking for would put you on a higher salary than your boss: these are all examples of situations in which the signs should be flashing out a warning to you. What you are aspiring to may be unattainable and, if you proceed, you will simply end up banging your head on a big brick wall. Banging your head on a brick wall is painful of course – it's something you should avoid doing!

At this point you may also find another sign flashing at you – this time one that's telling you to face up to facts and to look for a job somewhere else. How do you respond to this particular sign if it presents itself? The following short case study may provide the answer for you.

CASE STUDY: ISAAC

Isaac spent 12 years with a large retailing organization. He joined the company as a graduate trainee and, after a succession of promotions, he rose to the position of Area Manager in charge of eight stores. Two years ago Isaac started to have doubts about the competitiveness of his salary. Rumours had reached his ears about the kind of salaries other large retailers were paying – and this fuelled his determination to do something about his situation. What's more, Isaac's wife was expecting another child at the time, meaning they needed a larger house. It was these factors combined that gave Isaac the final push to start applying for other jobs.

After two months of sending off cvs and attending interviews, Isaac got an offer of employment from a small chain of health stores. The job was on very similar lines to the one he was doing already except the salary was 25% higher. There was the promise also of a further increase at the end of the year and, for these reasons, Isaac had little hesitation in writing off to accept.

As it turned out, however, Isaac found his new employers a very difficult bunch to deal with. The chain of health stores was family run and, unlike his previous bosses who were highly professional and well trained, the people Isaac now reported to seemed to have little idea about how to run an effective modern retail business. Conflict soon broke out over Isaac's plan to introduce a new stock control system. Isaac accused the Chief Executive of interfering and, from there on, the hostility between the two of them went from bad to worse. The culmination came six months ago when Isaac, feeling he could stand it no more, handed in his resignation. He had no other job to go to and found himself out of work for the first time in his life. Try as he did to find a position with comparable earnings, he was not successful. In the end, desperation and the need to have some money coming in forced him to accept a job as a manager of a small supermarket on something like half his previous salary.

Irrespective of how well you research prospective employers, changing jobs is intrinsically risky and most of us know this from our own experience. In the case of someone like Isaac, therefore, whose only grumble with his old firm seemed to be over pay, there was every reason to seek to resolve the pay issue internally first. So why didn't he think to do this? Let's ask him to explain.

> **Isaac:** 'The information from my sources led me to believe I could improve my salary by at least 20% on the outside market – which proved to be the case. As to my old firm, I felt there was no way I'd ever convince them to give me a 20% pay increase so what was the point in even asking?'

Whether or not Isaac was right in making this assumption we shall never know. However, the lesson from his case study is that, whilst shopping the outside job market intelligently is something we may all need to do from time to time, because of its intrinsic riskiness it should be seen as an action of *last* rather than *first* resort. This is particularly the case where the object of the exercise is simply to get a pay rise (i.e. where you have no other significant grievances against your employer).

> **Key point**
> Unless your profiling picks up some very negative readings about your employer's ability to pay, always be prepared to give them one last chance – who knows, you may even be pleasantly surprised with the result. On the other hand, if your bid doesn't work out (a) you will have lost nothing and (b) you won't see it as any failing on your part (it was the likely outcome anyway, so there is no reason for feeling dejected).

Sizing up your bargaining power

To sum up so far, you have:

- profiled your employer to determine their ability to pay you the increase you're seeking

■ identified situations in which the increase you are looking for may be very difficult or impossible to achieve, i.e. where bargaining won't work for you and where proceeding any further would be pointless.

Are you worth it?

Next we will turn to the other factor that will influence whether your bargaining is likely to lead to successful outcomes or not: what your employer thinks of you. In other words, in your employer's opinion, are you worth the figure you're asking for?

Given that many of us work for employers who operate formal appraisal systems, it is surprising to find how few people know what their bosses actually think of them. In this context we mean, whether their bosses view them as deserving cases for a pay rise.

Appraisal interviews are potentially flawed, of course. There is no guarantee that they will be conducted properly, in the same way that there is no guarantee that the words which flow across the desk will be totally frank. Indeed Casey's experience may be one that many of you share:

Casey: 'At my last appraisal interview the boss had a lot of nice things to say about my contribution to the success of the division and the quality of my work. But when I put in for a pay increase it was a totally different story. He gave me a big long list of my shortcomings and the improvements I would have to make before he could consider any adjustments.'

Your worth to your employer translates into your bargaining power and your bargaining power is what gives your case for a pay increase the clout it needs. It is therefore important to know what bargaining power is and how to use it. This is the subject we are going to look at next.

The nature of bargaining power

Bargaining power is a very **subtle** quantity. It can best be measured by asking yourself what pain you would inflict on your employer if, for any reason, you chose to up and leave. At one end of the scale would your boss be rubbing his or her hands with glee at the prospect of being shot of you? At the other end, would your skills and talents be sorely missed and difficult or impossible to replace?

Applying this 'leaver' test is quite useful because, when you think about it, at the back of your boss's mind, when deciding how to respond to your bid for a pay increase, will be the consequences if you decided to seek your fortunes elsewhere. Remember we used the word 'subtle' a few sentences ago? In these situations, the threat of leaving is one that is *implied* rather than *explicit*. The term **'silent bargaining power'** describes this situation and it is a term we will be using a lot from now on. Silent bargaining power is your leverage in pay bargaining situations.

Silent bargaining power

Let's now look a little more closely at the nature of silent bargaining power. There are strong links, obviously, between silent bargaining power and **job performance**. Someone who is a good performer clearly will be someone an employer wants to hang on to – and vice versa. Record of conduct also scores heavily. For example, if you are a trouble maker no one will be sorry to see you go. But there are other factors that also have a bearing on silent bargaining power and, to see how you rate, work your way through the following checklist and see how many of the questions you can put a 'yes' alongside.

- Do you have a scarce skill? If you do, then all other considerations apart, your employer is going to find you hard and potentially expensive to replace.
- Do you have some area of specialist knowledge that your employer places a high value on?
- Do you have contacts that are important to your employer's business? This is the usual source of bargaining power for people in sales.
- Are you privy to sensitive information about your employer's business – information that could be

damaging if it found its way into the wrong hands? Pricing structures come to mind here, as does any kind of information that is stock market sensitive.

■ Do you have knowledge of any technique or process that gives your employer a competitive edge?

■ Are you 'useful' to your employer? Do you put yourself out beyond the norms of what's normally expected of someone in your position?

Again, this list is by no means exhaustive but it will give you a clue about the kind of things that will give your case an extra bit of clout when it comes to presenting your pay bid to your employer.

What to do when your bargaining power is weak

What if you've not been able to say yes to any of the questions in the checklist? Where does this leave you?

Again, let's use a case study to add some real-life dimensions to the difficulties you face when you have little or no bargaining power. This is the tale of Rhoda.

CASE STUDY: RHODA

Rhoda is a 22-year-old design engineer who works in the design office of a large structural engineering company where she has been since she graduated from university 10 months ago. Rhoda feels she is being underpaid – a view she has formed after comparing salaries with two of her friends (two people who graduated at the same time as she did and who work for other companies). Rhoda realises, however, that she is still very much in a learner capacity and any work she does has to be checked carefully by her Section Leader. She fears, therefore, that she won't get much joy if she raises the question of her salary with the Design Manager.

Rhoda is right, of course. In fact, if she raises the question of her pay with her boss, she might find that she ends up with a flea in her ear – plus, perhaps, a sharp reminder that she is still largely a cost as far as the company is concerned.

Learners are just one category of people who don't have much in the way of bargaining power. Other examples are:

- people with limited skills
- people who, for one reason or another, have not been good job performers
- people with poor attendance records, including people with health problems
- people who have been in hot water over aspects of their behaviour
- people who are good performers but who hide their lights under a bushel
- people with skills that are plentiful in the market place and who will, therefore, be easy to replace
- sadly, people who are nearing retiring age.

The warning signal should be sounding out to anyone who falls into any of these categories. Their bargaining power is poor and, as a consequence, when it comes to negotiating a pay rise for themselves, their chances of success are low. In fact, rather like people working for employers who don't have the ability to pay, people with poor bargaining power might be well advised to back off. Once again, the chances are they'll end up banging their heads on that big brick wall.

So is this wiping off the pay aspirations of what must be a sizeable percentage of the population? Not quite. What you will notice about the factors that give people bargaining power is that many of them are *acquirable*. You can, for example, acquire more skills. You can become more useful to your employer. You can acquire specialist and valued areas of knowledge. How do you go about this? To start read the next chapter, 'Adding Value to Yourself'.

In Rhoda's case she is already acquiring skills that will one day greatly enhance her bargaining power. The advice to Rhoda, therefore, is 'bide your time'.

Setting your aim

We have reached the stage where you have decided that:

■ your employer has the ability to pay the increase you are looking for

■ you have some silent bargaining power that will give your case a bit of clout.

Now you have to decide the figure you want to name. How big an increase should you be looking for?

Any kind of bargaining starts with an aim. The aim in this case is a pay increase, but sometimes it's not easy to know what figure you should be putting on such a vague concept as your worth. For instance, could you be asking for too little? At the other extreme, could you be seen as being greedy? Alternatively, is the figure you have in mind roughly in line with what someone with your skills and experience ought to be paid?

When deciding what figure to go for, a good place to start is by asking yourself exactly where you're coming from. If you're not too sure about this, use the following checklist to see which of the four categories you fit into.

Category 1

■ Do you feel that your salary is below what someone with your experience and skills ought to be earning?

■ Does your employer lag behind when it comes to paying market rates, i.e. rates paid by other employers?

Category 2

■ Does the standard of your work and the level of effort you put in call for reward over and above the norm?

Category 3

■ Are the differentials between you and other members of staff fair and equitable?

■ Is the gap between you and the people who report to you wide enough to reflect your greater responsibilities?

Category 4
- ■ Do you need the money to finance additional expense in your personal life?
- ■ Are you thinking of buying a bigger house or sending your children to private schools?

There is no reason, of course, why you shouldn't be putting a tick alongside more than one of these categories. For example, someone who is being paid below market rates could also be someone who is experiencing differentials problems.

This bit of self-interrogation is to help you clarify, in your own mind at least, exactly what you are trying to achieve. This is important for two reasons:

1 You need to know what it's going to take to make you happy (this is important when it comes to evaluating the success of your bargaining).

2 At some point, someone may ask you to name your figure. You don't want to be put in the position of frantically trying to pluck one out of the air in the middle of an eyeball-to-eyeball meeting.

⚠ **WARNING!**

Whilst it is important to have a figure in mind *before* you start bargaining, it is a mistake to view this figure inflexibly. **Flexibility**, as we shall see later on, is very important in bargaining and you must seek to retain it at all times.

Are you going over the top?

This is a concern for many people. By asking for the figure you have in mind, will you be seen as being too greedy? Let's take another case study to explore this point a little further.

CASE STUDY: INA

Ina is a credit manager with a major wholesaler of children's clothing. Ina has had the feeling for some time that she is underpaid for what she does, but her 'evidence' is based largely on what her friends tell her about salaries in their companies and what she gleans from job advertisements for credit managers in the newspapers she reads. The indicators from these sources are that Ina should be looking for a substantial rise to bring her into line with market rates but what bothers her is what if she is wrong? In particular, she is concerned that she could come across as avaricious – something that will only serve to make her boss, the Chief Accountant, put the shutters up.

Ina is right to have concerns because going in with a bid that is patently over the top will only invite negative responses. Even more worrying is the fact it could put a dent in her credibility. On the other hand, if Ina really is being paid poorly for the responsibilities she is holding down, then asking for the right rate for the job is a perfectly reasonable request to make. What's more, employers who are paying poor salaries are usually well aware of the fact, so a request for a pay rise will come as no surprise to them.

But are the salaries Ina has seen in the newspapers or the hearsay information from her network of friends true reflections of the market rate? Or could it be that they represent just a narrow slice of the market – and the very top end of it at that? Could it be, therefore, that Ina's bid will be viewed as over the top by the Chief Accountant and dismissed out of hand as a consequence?

This is where Ina runs into the problem of not having all the information she needs to hand. The information in this case is data about the kind of salaries that someone with her skills and experience could expect to be paid on the open job market. So do we have any tips for Ina on how she could find out if her bid is reasonable or not? Here are two methods she could consider:

> 1 Ina could talk to a few employment agencies and find out from them what someone with her skills and

experience could expect to be paid on the outside job
market. Because of their business, employment
agencies are very much in touch with market rates.

2 Some jobs Ina sees advertised in the newspaper
(possibly the majority) won't contain any details of
salary. Instead there will be vague statements about
salary, like 'attractive' or 'negotiable' or 'commensurate
with the responsibilities'. Ina could apply for a few of
these jobs. If she gets interviews she will be able to find
out more about the salaries, thereby adding to her store
of knowledge about market rates.

NOTEPAD
Having a few job applications in the pipeline is not a bad thing
when you're involved in pay bargaining.

Deciding what you're going to say

Having satisfied yourself that you're not going over the top with
your pay bid and that the figure you have in mind is the right one to
be asking for, what you need to look at next is how you're going to
present your case. Presenting your case means having a word with
your boss and here there are two things going in your favour:

1 You know your boss – you know what kind of reception
your submission is likely to receive.

2 You know where decisions are made in your company
– meaning you know whether your boss has the
authority to give you a pay rise or whether they will
have to speak to someone higher up the ladder.

Timing your approach

This is important. There are clearly good times and bad times for
putting in a bid for more pay. Classic bad times include:

- when the boss is heavily preoccupied with some other matter, e.g. preparing budgets, in the throes of negotiating a big commercial contract or dealing with a crisis

- just after the salary review has taken place, i.e. when your boss is entitled to feel that the subject of salaries has been put to bed for a little while at least and when it might be quite difficult for your boss to justify any further tamperings (don't forget your boss usually has to answer to someone else on any changes to salaries)

- at the meeting to discuss your next year's salary (the decisions have already been taken and you've left it too late).

Conversely, a good time to make your approach is:

- when there are no other major distractions that will make the task of focusing your boss's mind difficult

- a few months in advance of the salary review.

Pick a moment when discussion won't be interrupted, particularly by telephone calls, or where it could be cut short because, say, one of you has to go to another meeting. For most of us, this means the best time for meetings to discuss pay is 'after hours'.

How to come across

First and foremost, it's important not to come across as a whiner because, as we all know, whiners don't get very far in life. Here is what you need to do:

- Don't say anything which could indicate that you are being driven by envy. Envy is a trademark of whiners, so do not make reference to the salaries of others (people your employers may not view as valid comparators anyway).

- Avoid accusations and accusatory language, e.g. 'You said you would do something about my pay last year but you never did.' Apart from being another trademark of whiners, accusations carry the double-edge liability of being viewed as potential threats. (Threats are the subject of the next section).

■ Whiners are people who like to air their pay grievances on every possible occasion. You can avoid the stereotype by confining your discussion to meetings arranged specifically for the purpose.

■ Whiners rarely point the way forward and this is because the whining is a way of life to them (something that serves its own ends). You can usually dispel any impression of whining by clearly stating the outcome you want (as you will be doing).

■ Whiners are never satisfied. If they're given what they want, they're usually back knocking on the door again before too much time has lapsed. This is a reason for making sure you don't understate your aims, i.e. don't ask for too little, then find later that it isn't enough.

NOTEPAD

Whining invites negative responses and this is why you will be taking great care not to say anything that could categorize you as a whiner.

Avoid making threats

One of the problems with making threats is that they seldom elicit the reaction you're looking for. Again, they invite negative responses from the person on the receiving end and, needless to say, this is an outcome you are very much seeking to avoid. In pay discussions the most commonly made threat is the threat to leave if the pay demand is not met. Let's use a case study to show how people who make threats to leave can sometimes come unstuck.

CASE STUDY: LIAM AND JANE

Liam is a sales negotiator and Jane is his boss. Liam is the top performer in the office as far as bringing in new business is concerned and he feels this calls for some extra recognition in his pay. He therefore raises the subject with Jane. Jane appears unsympathetic at first. She points out to Liam that he has not been with the company very long and still has much to learn. Feeling the last remark to be unjustified Liam retorts by telling Jane that, the way he sees it, his job performance is all that counts and, if Jane can't see her way to doing something about his salary, then he'll take his talents elsewhere. Taken aback, Jane replies to this by saying she doesn't respond to threats and if Liam feels he can do better by leaving the company then that's a matter entirely for him.

Reflecting on this meeting later, Liam realizes he's completely blown any chance he ever had of getting a pay increase. Of even greater concern to him now is the fact that he's put himself under pressure to carry out his threat to leave – either that or lose his credibility. What should he do? He likes the company really and feels he has good prospects. Leaving is not what he wants to do.

Words spoken in haste perhaps, but Liam has put himself in a position he didn't really want to be in. Jane didn't react to his threat in the way he expected and the response to his bid for more pay became totally negative. Whilst reflecting on what happened to Liam, you should consider the fact that you must never make threats unless you are prepared to carry them out.

If you go back to our earlier section about bargaining power, you will see that we emphasized the implicit use of bargaining power – hence the term *silent* bargaining power. What Liam attempted to do was to use quite *explicit* bargaining power by spelling it out to Jane exactly what would happen if he didn't get what he wanted. Jane, being no fool of course, didn't need this spelling out to her. She realized full well the consequences of saying no to Liam. The threat, in other words, was unnecessary but, once uttered, it had the unintended effect of forcing Liam down a path he didn't particularly want to go along.

The use of explicit bargaining power is a subject we will be exploring in more depth in Chapter 8, 'Blackmail'. At this juncture, suffice it to say, the use of explicit bargaining power is entering into high risk territory – something Liam found out to his cost. In short, and as we shall be seeing later, it is territory you only enter with your eyes wide open. Even then, you need to proceed with extreme caution.

NOTEPAD

Threats can be construed from other aspects of your behaviour that fall short of explicit words. Avoid the following therefore:

- raising your voice
- emotive language such as 'it's not fair' or 'I've had to suffer'
- aggressive body language, such as jabbing fingers or leaning across the desk.

How to make your case

Coming across as a whiner or trying to give force to your arguments by making threats are examples of bargaining postures that automatically invite negative responses. They are ones, therefore, that you should be seeking to avoid. But having dealt with the 'don'ts' of how to present a convincing case for a pay rise, let's now turn to the 'dos'. Here are a few guidelines on how to handle the meeting with your boss in a way that will invite *positive* responses:

- **Do** avoid complaints (e.g. 'The work I do here isn't recognized'). This will tend to throw your boss onto the defensive, which is not what you want.
- **Do** seek to reassure your boss by keeping everything you say within a positive framework, the general gist of

which should be 'I enjoy my job, I like working for the company and I see my future here...'. The misgivings about your pay need then to come across as your only gripe about the job, i.e. don't wrap it up with a lot of other grievances because (a) the point about your pay will lose its impact and (b) it could start to sound like whining.

■ **Do** say what you want to say as briefly and concisely as possible. Remember the more you ramble on, the greater the chances are of the message you're trying to get across not being understood properly or not being fully appreciated. Name the figure you're looking for and explain why you feel it's justified.

■ **Do** resist the urge to 'dress it up' with long meandering explanations and justifications. All that matters is you get your message across clearly.

■ **Do** leave it at that if you find you're getting a hostile reaction. Don't, whatever you do, get drawn into arguments because (a) it's a waste of energy and (b) it doesn't do anything to advance your case. Take the view that you're probably one step nearer to determining that your aspiration for a pay increase wasn't realizable in the first place. Allow, though, for the fact your boss may be having a bad day (you know the person). A polite exit line like 'I'll leave it with you to think over' could be the best tactic to use.

■ **Do** be ready for the boss to be noncommittal or saying something like 'Leave it with me, I'll get back to you'. This is usually coded language for meaning the decision on your pay rests with someone else (e.g. your boss's boss). Conversely, your boss may actually tell you that they need to speak to someone higher up the ladder.

■ **Do** be prepared not to get an instant answer. The likelihood of your boss agreeing to a pay increase on the spot is extremely remote (perhaps confined to situations where your boss is someone right at the top of the tree or the owner of the business).

■ Do prick up your ears for any feedback about how your boss views your pay prospects generally. This could be useful to you later on.

What you will have achieved in this meeting with your boss is as follows:

■ You've put your message across in clear and unequivocal terms.

■ You've been positive throughout, leaving your boss with the impression that pay is the only problem and that, if it can be resolved, then there are no other outstanding issues.

■ Your silent bargaining power will be starting to work for you.

Evaluating your success

Hopefully your pay bargaining will bring you the dividend you're looking for, but there are a number of other possible outcomes which are worth spending a few minutes pondering on.

The increase you're offered falls short

Whilst it would be silly and pointless to decline something that's been put on the table just because it doesn't come up to your expectations, you will have to decide whether to accept with good grace or on the basis that you only consider it in part settlement. The difference between the two is that 'good grace' means you drop the subject altogether whereas 'part settlement' means you'll go on pursuing your case for more money. With the latter, you will need to make this clear to your boss so that your silent bargaining power will go on working for you. How far short of your original figure the offer falls clearly has a bearing on which way this decision is going to go. Whilst it is important to remember the point about being flexible in your pay aspirations, it is equally wrong to let your employer go away with the impression that you have been bought off with a totally inadequate sum. What's more, the message you put across has to be consistent. You must be seen as someone who is totally credible – someone who means exactly what he or she says. (More on the subject of credibility soon.)

The increase is offered to you in another form

Here the potential variations are endless. For example, you could be offered a perk or the opportunity to earn more money by the introduction of a performance-related element into your pay package. What this might be flagging up is that the increase you're seeking is causing the company problems with differentials, i.e. giving you the increase to you in another form may be more palatable for them. Here again, don't be inflexible by confining your aspirations to advances in straight salary. Evaluate a perk for what it's worth (what it's worth to you, that is). See what you could earn from a performance-related bonus arrangement and, if in doubt, offer to try it out on a trial basis. Chapter 5 'Going onto Bonus', deals specifically with meeting pay aspirations by attaching some part of your remuneration package to a performance measure.

The increase can't be paid now – hang on a bit

Getting some commitment from your employer on *when* exactly they have in mind is likely to be difficult. It might be more helpful for you at this stage to find out why the increase can't be paid to you now. If it is because you still fall short of some defined standard (e.g. you need more experience in some aspect of your work) then proceed to the next subheading. If, on the other hand, the reasons are vague it is possible that the promise to pay up at some point in the future might be pie in the sky. What can you do about this? Not a fat lot at this stage, except to put a time limit mentally on how long you're prepared to wait for the pay increase to materialize (e.g. 12 months). If nothing's happened by then, take it that your bargaining has failed (your assessment of your employer's ability to pay was wrong).

The increase is attached to attainment of a goal

Again this is probably coded language for a differentials problem. The increase you're asking for would close the gap too tightly on people who have more skills and/or experience than you. Our advice? Take this at face value – at least until you have reason for viewing it otherwise. If you are lacking in skills and experience, then the company could be making a fair and reasonable point. If

Liam in our last case study hadn't botched his meeting with his boss by making threats he may well have found himself on the receiving end of an offer like this.

The importance of credibility

Credibility is a word that keeps cropping up. Credibility is important to you in internal bargaining situations because your employer must believe at all times that you are serious about what you are saying. Without this belief, your silent bargaining power won't work – meaning your chances of success will be severely impaired. Here is our advice on maintaining your credibility:

- You must be careful not to go over the top with the figure you name.
- You mustn't keep asking for pay increases, conveying the impression that you are the kind of person who is never satisfied.
- You must name your figure and stick to it.
- If you accept any less than the figure you've named, you must make the point that you're accepting it as 'part settlement'.

Credibility is what ensures your employer will pay attention to you when you ask for a pay increase. Anything that could damage your credibility should therefore be scrupulously avoided.

Questions and answers

Pay bargaining in stages – asking for some now and more later

Q *My employers are a pretty parsimonious lot, hence I predict fireworks if I put in for the 20% increase in my salary that I think I merit. What occurred to me, though, was that I might have more joy by asking for half now and another half in six months' time. What do you think?*

A Whilst we take the point that two small bites of the cherry might be easier for your employers to swallow than one big one, we have the slight worry that by asking for 10% increase now you could create the impression that this is the sum total of your ambitions. Hence, if you are successful and if your employer agrees to the increase, they might not react very favourably when you come knocking on the door again in six months' time. Apart from inviting a negative response, you could be putting a great big dent in your credibility – and possibly this is the part that worries us most. Our advice? Go in for the whole 20% now. If it's more palatable for your employer to pay it to you in two instalments then let the suggestion come from them. Equally, if they're only happy to pay you 10% then it's best you know about it sooner rather than later.

Using appraisals to raise pay issues

Q *We have twice-yearly appraisal interviews and it struck me that this was probably the ideal occasion for raising the subject of a pay rise with my employers. Do you agree?*

A Fine – providing your company is happy to include discussion of salary in appraisal interviews. Find out whether the appraisal interviews are being conducted end-on (i.e. with a number of staff one after the other). You could find discussion of your salary fore-shortened because the next appraisee is standing outside the door waiting to come in.

Going over the boss's head

Q *I recently asked for a rise and got turned down. My boss is notoriously bad in 'people situations' and he used his standard tactic of rejecting flatly everything that I had to say. I am now, therefore, considering whether to ask for a meeting with the Chief Executive in the hope that he will lend a more sympathetic ear to my plight. Given the difficulties of dealing with my boss, do you think this is a good idea?*

A We are sure we don't have to point out the risk in going over your boss's head, i.e. that it could inflict permanent damage on your relationship with him. Our advice? Appreciating your boss isn't the easiest person in the world to deal with, could you agree with him that bringing the CEO in on the discussions over your pay would be a move forwards? But what you mustn't rule out is that your boss may have already conferred with the CEO over your pay and the decision to turn you down is one they have arrived at jointly.

Receiving an offer and being asked to sign in full and final settlement

Q *In response to a long-running argument with my company about the level of my salary, I finally received an offer from them which falls a long way short of the figure I feel I need. To add further insult to injury they have told me that I would have to sign an agreement to say that I accept the increase offered to me as being in full and final settlement of all my grievances concerning pay – and I read into this that if I don't sign, the increase won't be payable. How do you suggest I handle this situation?*

A What you are being asked to do is unusual to say the least – in fact it's a device we've only ever seen used with the kind of individuals who ask for salary increases all the time and this begs the question, do you fall into this category? Hands up if you do because, the situation is then one you've brought on your own head. Putting in for pay increases is not something you should be doing repeatedly because, if you do, you will completely destroy your credibility and this is possibly what has happened. What to do? Accept the increase with good grace (sign the agreement) then see if you can mend your ways. On the other hand, if you don't fall into the category of being perpetually dissatisfied with your pay, it would seem reasonable to take issue with your company on why you're being asked to sign an agreement of this sort. At the end of the day if they really are a hard-headed bunch, perhaps the best advice is to be cynical and take what's on offer. Then proceed to see what the job market has to offer you.

Putting in for a higher figure than you really need

Q *Surely the best way to get a pay increase is to put in for a higher figure than you want, then let your employer beat you down. Why don't you suggest this?*

A For the simple reason that it will put a dent in your credibility. With the higher figure, no one will believe you're really serious and, by accepting the lower one, you will be proving the point. Take our tip: mean what you say when you enter into pay bargaining with your employer. Don't name a figure that's any more (or any less) than the one you are really seeking.

Working from home – problems with profiling

Q *I work from home, hence my knowledge of what's going on in the company is pretty minimal – meaning it's difficult for me to carry out a profiling exercise along the lines you suggest. Any ideas? Should I be comparing notes with colleagues, for example i.e. other home based people like myself?*

A Picking the brains of colleagues on subjects such as what they know about internal pay structures might strike them as odd. What's more, it opens up the possibility of your enquiries getting fed back into the wrong ears – namely those of your boss. This could lead to problems – not what you want when you are preparing to enter into a negotiation about your salary. Our advice? Proceed with the information you've got, however inadequate. If your pay bargaining hits a brick wall because of some factor outside your (limited) sphere of knowledge take this account. In other words, don't see the failing as a reflection on you or the way you went about things.

New member of staff on higher salary than you

Q *Quite by chance I found out that someone taken on recently is on a higher salary than me and, to add insult to injury, I am now being asked to show this person the ropes. How am I supposed to react to this situation? Taking your point about never making reference to the salaries of others, how else do I get fair treatment for myself?*

A What your experience reflects is the difficulties of attracting people on the open market and sometimes having to pay them higher salaries than existing staff to make it worthwhile for them to move. None of this makes the situation any more palatable for you, of course, but one way of looking at it is that your employer clearly has the ability to pay better salaries meaning the door is wide open to you to try out your silent bargaining power. This will be all the more effective if (a) you don't put yourself across as a whiner and

(b) you are seen to be giving your new colleague full support and cooperation.

Too old

Q *I am 59 and my understanding of what you are saying is that by virtue of this fact alone I won't have much in the way of silent bargaining power. Is this correct?*

A Not quite. You may for example have some scarce skill that your employer would find hard to replace. Equally, you may have all kinds of know-how locked up inside your head. Where people in the last 10 years of their working lives do occasionally fall down, however, is with their credibility – in short, their employers don't believe they would ever leave and this puts a serious dent in their silent bargaining power. If you think this applies to you, read what we have to say about being part of the furniture in Chapter 3.

Summary

Bargaining works where:

- ■ your employer has the ability to pay
- ■ your silent bargaining power is strong
- ■ you don't do anything to dent your credibility (e.g. by going in with over-the-top demands)
- ■ you state your ambitions clearly and succinctly so your employer knows exactly where you're coming from
- ■ you avoid negative bargaining postures, such as whining and making threats
- ■ you retain your flexibility, meaning you listen carefully to any alternative suggestions your employer puts forward

Unless your profiling suggests you'll be achieving nothing except banging your head on a brick wall, seeking to come to an agreement with your employer is certainly what you should be trying first. If it doesn't work, then you will have learned a great deal about your employer's ability to pay and your silent bargaining power (important for what follows).

Verdict on bargaining

Good points

View bargaining as the method of first resort. It commends itself as being low on risk and silent bargaining power can be used to its best effect (your employer knows the cost of losing you).

Bad points

There is potential for you to be banging your head on a brick wall if either (a) your employer doesn't have the ability to pay or (b) your bargaining power is weak (e.g. if you have blotted your copy book for any reason).

2 | ADDING VALUE TO YOURSELF

Silent bargaining power is *acquirable*. This is what Chapter 2 is all about – adding value to yourself and, as a consequence, enhancing your ability to strike good pay deals with your employer. We will look at:

- Factors that give weight to silent bargaining power – the assets you need to acquire to give your case that extra bit of clout
- The importance of image (your Lifelong Interview)
- Adding to your skills and experience – how to go about it
- Adding to the contribution you make to the work of the team
- 'Cornering' areas of skill and knowledge – making yourself indispensable (the ultimate exercise in silent bargaining power)

Constituents of silent bargaining power

In the last chapter we saw silent bargaining power as the agent that will tip the scales for you in negotiations over pay. If you've got it, your employer is far more likely to accede to your bid. If you haven't, the likelihood is your employer will say no.

It is a mistake, however, to see silent bargaining power as a static quantity. Like a lot of other things in life, it comes and goes and, to a large extent, this coming and going is under your control. For example, if you don't keep up with the latest developments in your trade or profession, your skills will depreciate and your silent bargaining power will suffer as a result.

Let's start, however, by looking at the factors that have a bearing on silent bargaining power – what should you be focusing on if you want to give yourself that extra bit of muscle in your dealings with your employer?

■ **Your skills base** – someone with a wide range of skills clearly has more value to an employer than someone whose skills are limited and narrow. In particular, those who have acquired sought-after and scarce skills have a lot going for them in terms of silent bargaining power.

■ **Your experience** – again, a person with a lot of know-how or extensive contacts is going to be someone with a great deal of silent bargaining power. If the know-how extends into confidential areas of the employer's business (e.g. trade secrets) then this silent bargaining power is amplified many times over.

■ **Your ability as a team player** – someone who contributes to the work of the team, someone who is a linchpin in the organization, someone who is always prepared to offer a willing pair of hands is probably an employee who has a lot of silent bargaining power. Key team players are people who are sorely missed when they leave.

■ **Your track record and performance** – someone who is conscientious and hardworking will be viewed as an asset to an employer, whereas someone who is lazy and troublesome will not. Silent bargaining power accrues, therefore, in people who can project a **work-perfect/ person-perfect** image.

NOTEPAD

Striving to attain a work-perfect/person-perfect image means attaching the trademark of excellence to everything you do, both in your work and the way you conduct yourself in your dealings with others. Never let these standards lapse for any reason and always try to be the best.

Getting your image right

Picking up on the last of these bullet points, we need little reminding that we live in an image conscious world where the way we come across has a great deal to do with how successful we are. Nowhere is this truer than with silent bargaining power. The image we project to our employers is all important in leading them to a positive view of our worth.

The Lifelong Interview

Those of you who have read any of our other books or have been present at any of our teach-ins will already be familiar with the Lifelong Interview. But for those of you who haven't, the gist of it is outlined below.

When we go to job interviews we are very conscious of the image we project:

■ We take care over our appearance.

■ In our answers to questions we make great effort to put ourselves across in the best possible light.

■ Any flaws we have are kept well out of sight.

Not so, of course, in our day-to-day dealings with our employers. We are less mindful of our image and occasionally some of our bad points slip out. The difficulty is, of course, we are talking about projecting an image day-in, day-out over a long period of time, whereas a job interview lasts, on average, about 45–60 minutes.

The message? The kind of gloss you previously saved up for interviews should be the kind of gloss you put on every day – hence the term 'Lifelong Interview'. The spin-offs are not only in terms of bettering your silent bargaining power but also in other important areas of managing your career, such as enhancing your ability to network effectively with others.

NOTEPAD

Here are a few pointers for putting the Lifelong Interview into practice:

- Don't have off days.
- Keep your appearance up to scratch at all times.
- Be helpful to others and do your best for them.
- Never whinge or whine.
- Don't run down your colleagues and bosses behind their backs.
- Don't blame others for your mistakes – if it's your fault, own up to it.
- Keep your flaws to yourself.
- Give your best to every day.
- Seek to project a work-perfect/person-perfect image at all times.

Adding to your skills base and experience

CASE STUDY: RICK, JAKE AND GLYN

Rick is a manufacturing engineer. Rick works for a medium-sized engineering company that produces precision-machined components for the aerospace and automotive industries. Over recent years Rick's company has invested heavily in state-of-the-art, computer-controlled machine tools and, with the arrival of each item of new equipment, Rick has made a point of learning how to use the programming software. He is now in the unique position of knowing how to program every machine in the factory – plus, he can fault find when problems with software arise.

Rick has been concerned about his salary for some time, feeling it doesn't reflect the market rate for someone with his skills and talents. Two weeks ago he had a word with his boss Jake, and Jake immediately went to see Glyn, the Chief Executive.

Glyn's view at first was that Rick would have to wait for the salary review at the end of the year. Then Jake pointed out the downside if Rick were to decide to leave. Notably, they'd be left in the hands of the machine manufacturers every time a program went wrong and the cost consequences of having to call in service engineers could be enormous. It all went to prove, as Jake pointed out, that Rick was an extremely useful person to have around. Keeping him happy was definitely in the company's best interests.

The points to pick out of this case study are as follows:

- ■ Rick acquired silent bargaining power by extending his skills base.
- ■ He did this entirely of his own volition.
- ■ His silent bargaining power worked for him when he put in for a pay rise (the problems that would accrue to the company in the event of him leaving were at the forefront of his boss's mind).

But what if Rick was the kind of person who was always whinging about his pay? Would the silent bargaining power have worked for him in quite the same way?

We suspect not. Indeed we suspect his bosses would have viewed his approach in an entirely different light (yet another try-on). This emphasizes again one of the central messages in Chapter 1 – that, to work for you, silent bargaining power has to be backed by credibility. Your bosses have to believe you're serious otherwise they won't react in the way you want them to.

NOTEPAD

You will have noticed how a lot of the lessons in the book are starting to join up. Note, in particular, the strong links between silent bargaining power, credibility and the work-perfect/person-perfect, non-whinging, non-whining image (the lesson of the Lifelong Interview).

Here are some more examples of people who are adding value to themselves:

- ■ **Trudi** works for a company with expanding global markets and is learning two foreign languages in her spare time.

- ■ **Sasha** has persuaded her company to sponsor her to do an MBA.

- ■ **Grant**, the Chief Accountant of a company, is now running the Purchasing Department in addition to his own (the Purchasing Manager was axed in a headcount-slashing exercise 6 months ago).

The last of these examples (Grant) is interesting because it illustrates that opportunities to add value to yourself often arise from situations that, on the face of it, seem 'bad'. In Grant's case, he was asked to take on more responsibility for no extra pay. At the time he agreed reluctantly (he already had enough on his plate running the Accounts Department). But, by successfully combining two functions, Grant has now boosted his worth to his employer and, as a consequence, his silent bargaining power. The pay back will come next time he puts in for a rise.

NOTEPAD

In the down-sized, delayered, restructured, headcount-slashing world we live in today there are plenty of situations like Grant's. See if you can spot a few in your own organization. See what opportunities exist for broadening your skills base and experience and adding value to yourself.

Reap what you sow

There is an important side issue here. What you put into an organization usually equates to what you get out of it, and this applies as much to pay as to anything else. A common mistake a lot of people make is that, when opportunities for adding to their value come up, they miss out by asking for the money up front. Here is another case study to show what we mean.

CASE STUDY: DEXTER AND JILL

Dexter works in the customer service department at a branch of a large vehicle leasing business. The department has been hit by a spate of leavers, meaning that everyone is having to work at full stretch until replacement staff can be found and trained.

One night after work, Dexter's boss Jill asks him to stay behind so she can have a word with him. She has been thinking of reorganizing the office, she tells him, and one of the changes she wants to make is to put someone in charge of key accounts – the person she has in mind being Dexter. Dexter hesitates. What about the money? he asks. Jill shakes her head. She can't do anything about the money just at the moment, she explains. She was really rather hoping Dexter would take the job on the basis of the extra experience it would give him (up to now Jill has handled most of these key accounts herself).

Dexter isn't very happy with this answer because he's been concerned about his pay for some time. He asks, therefore, for time to think Jill's suggestion over. Jill agrees and says she will speak to him again next day.

Later that evening, Dexter reflects on the conversation with Jill. The more he thinks about it, the more he sees it that Jill is trying to offload her work on him and do it on the cheap. No, he says to himself, if Jill wants him to take on more responsibility then she will have to pay him the proper wage.

Jill is clearly constrained at the moment in what she can do for Dexter pay-wise (a situation a lot of managers find themselves in when it comes to reorganizing responsibilities). If Dexter sticks to his decision to dig his heels in, the likely outcome is that Jill will find someone else to take on the new key accounts role. Dexter will, therefore, miss out on the chance to add value to himself – his only gain being the worthless bit of self-satisfaction he got from feeling he's made some kind of point. The message? Grasp these opportunities to add value to yourself with both hands. Never lose sight of the main aim by focusing too closely on short-term gains. Avoid this kind of myopia at all costs because, as in Dexter's case, you could miss out on opportunities to make major advances in your silent bargaining power.

Becoming a good team player

In any organization there are key figures – people who provide a focal point for their peers, people around whom the rest of the team revolves. By definition, such people carry a lot of weight as far as their employers are concerned. Such people would be sorely missed if they left and, therefore, tend to find they get a far more sympathetic ear when it comes to bargaining a pay rise for themselves.

How do you make yourself into a key team player? The answer harps back to the lesson of the Lifelong Interview:

■ You must always strive to be someone who gives their best (every day).

■ You must be supportive of your colleagues – help them if they need help, give your time to them freely, make yourself into the kind of person who others come to for advice and guidance.

■ Don't run people down behind their backs – be seen as someone who is fair-minded and nonjudgemental.

■ If you've got strong or controversial opinions, keep them to yourself.

■ Don't form likes and dislikes for people – as far as you can, treat everyone the same.

Cornering areas of skill and knowledge

If you like, this is the ultimate exercise in silent bargaining power: making yourself into a unique quantity; making yourself practically indispensable; making the prospect of you leaving into a total disaster for your employer.

What's involved?

Cornering skills and knowledge often comes about accidentally and our friend Rick (page 33) is a possible example. From what we know of Rick, it doesn't seem very likely that he set out intentionally to become the only person in the factory who could sort out the software faults on computer-controlled machine tools. But given this uniqueness, his silent bargaining became enormous. If he handed his notice in, his employer would be left with three stark choices:

1 To train someone else to become proficient with the software

2 To recruit someone from the outside

3 To rely on the back-up service of machine tool manufacturers.

Bringing someone else on-stream with specialized software skills would take time and, cost money. Recruiting someone new would probably involve paying a high salary (sufficient to attract them). Relying on service engineers would also be, as Rick's boss Jake pointed out, an expensive option. Plus there would be the hassle of getting engineers to come in (or what would seem like a hassle to a company used to having the expertise on-tap and in-house). The easier route? To keep Rick sweet by paying him the figure he is asking for.

Here are some more people who have unintentionally cornered areas of skill and know-how:

- **Meg** is the only person in the office who can converse in Russian (her company has recently acquired two Russian clients).

- **Bal** knows the complex wage payment system used by his company inside-out (everyone else is completely baffled by it).

- **Melissa** has acquired a specialist knowledge of international employment law (her company regularly sends people on two-year overseas postings).

These examples also help to illustrate that areas of skills and knowledge which people manage to corner are often ones that appear formidable to the average person's mind. Imagine how you would feel if you had to acquire the area of skill or know-how yourself, e.g. learn a difficult foreign language, delve into the arcane workings of a complicated wage structure, spend your time reading up on dry subjects such as international employment law etc.

NOTEPAD

See if you can identify any areas of specialist skill and know-how in your own organization. What would it take for you to develop the expertise yourself? Don't be put off by the weightiness of the subject. Remember the more difficult it looks, the less likely it is you will ever have to face any challengers. See the benefits in terms of the value you add to yourself and the accrual of tremendous silent bargaining power.

Keeping skills and know-how to yourself

This brings us neatly to the darker side of acquiring areas of unique skill and knowledge: how to keep it to yourself – in short, how to keep your massive, silent bargaining power intact.

Since hogging skills and know-how flies directly in the face of the modern concept of the knowledge-based organization and knowledge sharing, it is an aim which is not going to be easy to achieve. Smart employers actively seek to prevent individuals cornering areas of skill and knowledge, so you have to rely on the inertia which is prevalent in many organizations (employers may be happy to go along with your cornering because it makes for a quiet life). Naturally, though, the minute you put in for a pay increase, this acts as a sharp reminder that you've got them over a barrel. If they've got any sense, they'll be making sure they're not ever going to be put in the same position again. In Rick's case, Glyn, the Chief Executive, will surely be asking Jake why no one else in the business has got an insight into programming the machine tools.

The upshot? Exercising massive doses of silent bargaining power derived from cornered areas of skill and know-how, is usually a one-off event. Next time, the company will see to it that it isn't caught in quite the same way again. Someone else will be trained up, so your skill and know-how will no longer be unique and your silent bargaining power will be diluted as a result.

Key point

If you're in the position of having unique skills and/or know-how, make the most of the situation while you can.

NOTEPAD

It won't have escaped your attention that, by adding value to yourself in the eyes of your employer, you are also adding value to yourself in the eyes of the wider job market. What this means is that the stakes are raised. Your employer will be even more aware that, if they can't provide you with what you want, there will be plenty of others happy to oblige.

Small firms

A lot of people now work in small firms where, on the face of it, the opportunities for extending skills and broadening experience seem to be limited by the size of the operation. But is this necessarily the case? Here are two examples that suggest otherwise:

- **Clare** works as secretary/PA in a small consultancy specializing in environmental monitoring. In addition to her usual duties, Clare also deals with the accounts of the business – a job she took over from one of the partners 18 months ago.

- **Simon** is a trainee solicitor with a small, family law practice. Recently the practice decided to acquire a new computer system and, because he has good IT skills, Simon was given the task of overseeing its implementation.

What these examples illustrate is that job boundaries in small firms are often very flexible and willing pairs of hands can have all sorts of tasks placed in them, thus opening up possibilities to those seeking to add value to themselves. In Clare's case, it is clear that she has far more worth to her business as a 'Jill of All Trades' than she would have had if she'd remained a plain secretary/PA. If she had the need, the leverage she could exert on her employers in the form of silent bargaining power would probably be quite formidable. The message? If you work in a small business don't miss the opportunity it offers for extending your skills base and broadening your experience. The magic words are 'I can do that – leave it to me.'

NOTEPAD

Decentralized organizations (large employers who have opted for simpler, more devolved systems of management) often end up as businesses within businesses (virtual small firms). These employers provide all sorts of opportunities for adding value by extending skills and broadening experience. We shall see more of this later on in the book.

Questions and answers

The Lifelong Interview – 'My past history is against me'

Q *My track record with my company has been patchy to say the least. Two years ago I went through a bad spell following the break-up of a long-term relationship and I made the mistake of letting it affect my work. The result was a warning to get my act together or else, and this had the desired effect of making me pull up my socks and mend my ways. I still feel my past lapses are being held against me and I wonder whether I can ever succeed in wiping the slate clean. In short, if I tried adding value to myself would I be wasting my time? I ask the question because my pay isn't progressing as well as I would like and this is an issue I need to address.*

A Though it's never too late to turn over a new leaf, we do take the point you're making, because silent bargaining power depends on your employer's overall opinion of you. If this isn't good and if they would be quite happy to see the back of you, then no amount of adding value to yourself is going to help you to coax them into giving you a big rise. Our suggestion? Make your case (you've got nothing to lose) but if all you get is a stream of negatives take it to mean your silent bargaining power is weak (as you suspect) and, therefore, pay bargaining isn't going to work for you. Sooner or later you're going to have to form a judgement on whether this employer is ever going to deliver – whether in fact you might be better off making your fresh start somewhere else. This is a decision for you of course. All we would say is, don't let pay grievances fester for too long because they become the stuff of bitterness and resentment.

How can I add to my value when I only work part-time?

Q *I work part-time (mornings only) so I don't see what scope I have for adding to my value. Is this really for me?*

A Look at it this way. Silent bargaining power isn't the preserve of people who work full-time or, for that matter, people who fit into any particular category. Where this gets confusing, however, is where part-time equates to low skills – as it often tends to. People with low skills don't have much in the way of silent bargaining power, as we have seen, and this applies irrespective of whether they're full-time or part-time. Conversely, in pay terms, those with few skills probably have most to gain from acquiring the skills they don't have currently.

No opportunities for acquiring skills

Q *My company has a very negative attitude towards training. Last year I put in a request to go on a 2-day course in IT skills. The answer I got back was no, because they felt it had no relevance to my work. Given this negative attitude, how am I supposed to add to my value?*

A Book two days' holiday and go on the IT course in your own time. Alternatively, you may find the same course is available at times when you are not at work (e.g. in the evenings). The serious point is that this is about managing your own career. Don't expect employers to do the job for you because very often you'll end up disappointed.

Home based

Q *I work from home and, as I see it, I don't have any opportunities for adding to my experience and skills. Have I got this right or is there something I'm missing?*

A As a rule people who work at home enjoy greater freedom meaning they have more opportunities for going on courses and/or pursuing programmes of self-study than the average nine-to-five, sitting-at-a-desk person. With the internet opportunities for learning at home have never been better.

Too much to do already

Q *My working day is frantic enough as it is without taking on any more responsibilities. How do I add to my value when I don't have the time?*

A If you're as busy as you say you are then your silent bargaining power may be in need of enhancing. Be careful though that you're not just using 'too busy' as an excuse for doing nothing (only you know the answer to this).

Summary

Silent bargaining power is perhaps the most effective force at your disposal when it comes to going after pay rises and this is why it is always worth trying to acquire as much of it as you possibly can. Given that the obstacle to making progress on the pay front is frequently lack of skills and/or experience, the obvious path to go along is to try to add some. If, however, the obstacle is your employer's inability to deliver the pay rise you are after, no amount of adding to your value is going to change the situation – and this is why it is so important to establish an ability to pay at the outset. Not only must you do your initial profiling properly, but you must also read the signs as you go through the various stages of bargaining – particularly signs that suggest you could have got your initial profiling wrong.

Having said this, adding to your value is always going to work in your favour eventually. So, to an extent, it is something you should be seeking to do anyway, irrespective of any designs you may have on getting a pay increase. If you do find you have to go out onto the open job market to fulfil your aspirations, the more skills and experience you have to offer, the easier it will be for you to get what you are looking for.

Verdict on adding value to yourself

Good points

Adding to personal value is a natural extension to bargaining. Plus it will stand you in good stead if you should ever have to shop the outside job market. In short, anything you do under this heading has got good spin-offs.

Bad points

Disappointing if it doesn't work out. It seems like a lot of effort for nothing.

3 | BEING THE BEST

Excellence is something you should always be striving for. It has immense silent bargaining power and in this chapter we will be looking at how to exercise the power of excellence to best effect – how to cash in on being good at your job; how to get the financial recognition that star performers deserve. Our topics include:

■ Subjective judgements and the problem of forming assessments of job performance – where you and your boss need to be seeing eye-to-eye

■ Pay rises based on merit – how being the best converts into hard currency

■ Visibility – getting the work-perfect/person-perfect image across in the right quarters and selling the message where it counts

■ Making internal networks work for you – letting others sing your praises on your behalf

Measuring excellence

Being the bee's knees at work might seem to guarantee that our employers will look after us and do everything necessary to keep us happy. But this isn't always the case – a fact many of us will be able to testify to from our own experience. What goes wrong? Let's ask Qurban to tell us what he thinks:

> **Qurban:** 'I've been with this company for 16 years. I have had more experience than anyone else in the office and the proof of how good I am is the fact that all new starters are put with me to

> make sure they learn how to do the job properly. It's a pity though that none of this is recognized when it comes round to salary review time. All I ever seem to get is the standard rations. To me this shows the company doesn't value its people properly. Really, it's typical of the way they go on.'

Silent bargaining power not working? Or, as Qurban suggests, a company incapable of identifying its own high performers? Or something else perhaps? For the answer, let's ask Jacqui, Qurban's boss.

> **Jacqui:** 'Qurban? Ok, he's somebody I can live with but he'll never set the world on fire. We put new starters with him for the simple reason it doesn't hold back other people in the office who are capable of working at twice his speed.'

What this illustrates is how easy it is to pick up false readings about your worth to your employer. What Qurban took as a positive testimony to his excellence (being picked to show the ropes to new starters) had, in fact, the opposite meaning to the one he read. It is important to appreciate the possibility of making false readings because they can lead you to make false assumptions about the strength of your silent bargaining power. For instance, if Qurban puts in for a big pay rise, his boss Jacqui probably won't view it with too much sympathy. The chances are that Qurban will come away empty handed and with the negative opinions he already holds about his company largely confirmed. Qurban will then be further down the road that leads to embitterment, whereas what he should be doing is addressing the problem by pulling his finger out and getting his job performance up to the same standard as his colleagues.

What's the lesson here? Simply this: putting a measure on your own excellence is riddled with potential problems. Don't jump to too many big conclusions about your worth to your employer in job performance terms. If bargaining doesn't work for you, you should allow for the fact you may be taking wrong readings. Back off and, by using the checklist on pages 5 and 6, see if you can put your finger on where the problem may lie.

One person's view of another

Here's an interesting experience which some of you may share.

CASE STUDY: BURT

Burt spent his first 5 years working for a publisher of trade journals where he regularly received poor performance reviews from his boss. He then moved to his current employer (another publishing company) where his new boss seems to have a totally different opinion of him. Burt is now doing well. On the strength of his performance, he has been ear marked for promotion and his salary is going up in leaps and bounds.

At the end of the day, evaluation of performance is largely one person's view of another and, because of this, it is subject to the whole range of interpretations that can and do creep into human relationships. You can hit it off with one boss but find it difficult ever to see eye-to-eye with another – and your silent bargaining power goes up or down as a consequence. Any judgements you make, therefore, about the strength of the hand you are playing must be viewed in the context of your relationship with your current boss.

Visibility

In itself, being the best may not be enough to get you the rise you want. You must also be *seen* to be the best and this is an entirely different kettle of fish.

We scarcely need reminding that we live in an image-conscious world where appearances often count for more than the real substance of things underneath. Not that we would recommend you attempt to portray yourself as anything other than what you really are, but there is a need, always, to ensure that the image you're projecting is in sufficiently sharp focus to ensure you're not falling into the trap of hiding your light under a bushel.

Image management is a subject we touched on in Chapter 2. There we talked about the Lifelong Interview and how important it is to give your best to every day. What we want to do now is ensure that this effort doesn't all go to waste. We want to make sure that people who can influence pay outcomes for you are fully aware that you're the best thing since sliced bread. This is where your *visibility* comes in.

Having a sufficiently high profile in your organization is important because the excellent job you're doing needs to be seen by people who matter. In theory this shouldn't be too difficult because the person you want to impress is usually your immediate boss, i.e. someone you have day-to-day dealings with and who will be fully aware of the standard of your work. The problems tend to creep in where:

- your boss is not the person who can influence pay outcomes for you; the decisions are made by someone higher up the ladder
- where the value of your input is overlooked (this being a common problem with people who have been with organizations for a long time)
- where you are removed from the centres of decision-making – as is the case with peripatetics and people who work from home (teleworkers).

These are all situations in which the strength of your silent bargaining power may not be getting through to where it needs to be brought to bear – and hence it doesn't work. In other words these are situations that call for 'something special' .

Image by association

People who don't have day-to-day dealings with you form their impressions, not just from the fleeting occasions they come into contact with you, but also from the associations that mention of your name conjures up in their minds.

CASE STUDY: PAOLO, JOSH AND LARRY

Paolo is the Sales Manager of a company which provides a range of hygiene and sanitation services to a wide spectrum of commercial users. Paolo's sales force consists of 40 account executives scattered nationwide, mostly people who work from home and people he only sees on occasions such as new product launches and at the twice-yearly sales conferences. Other than this, he maintains contact with them by fax or e-mail.

Two of Paolo's account executives are Josh and Larry. Both of them pull in reasonable sales but, in Paolo's eyes, two people could hardly be any more different. Josh always has his reports in on time, whereas Larry usually has to be chased. Josh is meticulous about replying to his faxes and e-mails, whilst Larry invariably has to be sent several reminders. Paolo views Josh, therefore, as someone who is organized, business-like and efficient. Larry, on the other hand, he sees as a lackadaisical type to whom 'anything goes', i.e. not a person he would particularly wish to rely on.

What we can safely deduce from this case study is that Josh's silent bargaining power is several notches up on Larry's – and, when it comes to asking for pay rises, there are no prizes for guessing who will come out on top!

Whether Josh is being intentionally smart or not, he is succeeding in manipulating his image by association. In Paolo's mind he is associated with good points – namely getting his reports in on time and replying to his faxes and e-mails. With Larry, however, the association is with bad points (failing on both counts). Pretty quickly these associations convert into overall views of each person's worth to the business – even though sending in reports and responding to faxes and e-mails probably only constitutes a tiny and relatively unimportant part of being the totally effective account executive. The trick, therefore, is to spot these essential areas (however trivial they may be) and make sure you excel in them. The associations will then work for you and this has special relevance to those who need to make impressions on distant figures such as:

- remote figures in geographical terms (like Paolo)
- remote figures, because they're several rungs up the management ladder from where you're sitting
- remote figures who're remote because that's the way they behave.

Teleworkers and peripatetics

The last case study highlights the difficulties faced by people who work away from base when it comes to having to negotiate better pay deals for themselves. The exercise of silent bargaining power is made less easy by the fact that they are not sitting there in the office, an ever present reminder of their worth to the organization. Sadly, out of sight frequently means overlooked.

Helped by technology, the trend in recent years has been towards having fewer and fewer people based in large and expensive office suites. Armed with mobile phones, lap-top computers, and various types of messaging devices, people can work either on the hoof (touching base only occasionally and perhaps sharing a 'hot' desk), from their own homes or, in some cases, from one-person offices.

This may make for an interesting life but it's not all good news, particularly when the task in hand is trying to negotiate a better salary for yourself:

1 Profiling your company is made that much harder by being away from the scene of the action. You don't get to hear what's buzzing round on the grapevine; you're the last to detect changes in culture arising, for example, out of the arrival of a new Chief Executive; you miss out on all those vital snippets of information that are so useful in forming views on how companies are performing and, last but not least, because you don't know anyone, tapping into internal networks won't be an option that is available to you.

2 It's harder to articulate your pay ambitions to a boss who (a) you don't know particularly well and (b) you can only speak to over the 'phone.

3 Adding value to yourself by extending your skills and broadening your experience is difficult when you're isolated from other functions in the company.

4 As we have seen, bringing your silent bargaining power to bear is made harder because your face is not constantly in the frame (lack of visibility).

If you're a teleworker or if, for other reasons, the nature of your job separates you from the centres of activity in your company, then you may need to consider the following:

■ As we saw in the answer to one of the questions at the end of Chapter 1, your employer profiling needs to have greater margins for error. For example, if you find your employer completely hard-nosed when it comes to bargaining better pay arrangements, take this as a clue to the fact that you haven't picked up the full story as far as the organization's culture is concerned. Don't, however, see this as a reflection on you. Rather, view the experience as a learning exercise. You've just proved, perhaps, that your company won't ever deliver on pay, i.e. bargaining won't work for you and, that by proceeding any further, you will be banging your head on a brick wall.

■ You may have to go into pay negotiating with little or no idea of the reaction you are going to get from your boss. Again, allow that margin of error.

■ Being away from an office situation has some advantages – notably, you have greater freedom in the way you allocate your time. This could be useful, for example, if you should decide to pursue some course of training or further education that is not specifically relevant to your current employment.

■ See what you can do to develop internal networks in your company (networking is a subject we will be looking at shortly). You will find having voices that can speak up for you and ears that can listen out enormously beneficial when it comes to bargaining a better deal for yourself.

Part of the furniture

A few pages back we gave a mention to the characters who form the backbones to most companies. Typically long-serving and typically underpaid, they are the unsung heroes and heroines who rarely get mentioned in despatches and never get a look in on the medal parade.

CASE STUDY: SAMUEL

Samuel has been with his company for nearly 20 years and during most of this time he has been a member of the company's superannuation scheme. Samuel also has a number of long-service perks such as 3 days' extra holiday and a preferential loan arrangement which he used to finance an extension to his house 3 years ago. Samuel has been feeling for some time that his salary does not reflect the fact that he is practically carrying everyone else in the department. Indeed, with some jobs that come in, he is the only person who is competent to deal with them. What continues to sadden Samuel, though, is the way he's always passed over when the time for giving out rises comes round. Sure, he gets the standard few per cent just the same as everyone else does but, in his view, this is hardly recognition for the high standard of his work and the long hours he has to put in. A few weeks ago he put these points to his boss but the reaction he got was not very encouraging.

On the face of it, this is someone with substantial silent bargaining power but for some reason it doesn't seem to be working. So what's going wrong for Samuel? Why isn't his boss immediately forking out whatever extra cash it will take to make him happy? Indeed, is Samuel like Qurban a few pages back (someone who has taken a false reading of his own worth)?

Sadly there are some people – long-serving people in the main – who begin to get treated as part of the furniture and, at a rough guess, this is what has happened in Samuel's case. Silent bargaining power doesn't work for these people for the simple reason that their employers don't believe they're capable of leaving. The effect on their superannuation, the loss of their perks, the fear of having to say goodbye to familiar surroundings and faces and the terror of taking the step into the big outside world – these are all sufficient deterrents, at least in their employers' eyes. In short, the problem for people like Samuel is one of credibility: they are viewed as part of the furniture because no one takes them seriously.

The answer? It's not going to be easy but Samuel somehow has to convince his employers that he is someone who needs to be taken seriously. Somehow the message has got to sink in that, if Samuel doesn't get what he wants, he could well go off and seek his fortunes elsewhere.

How to do this? One suggestion is to take the bull by the horns – to say that you feel you've become part of the furniture and how, in your eyes, this has affected the way in which your salary has progressed; to say also how unfortunate it would be both for the company and yourself if you ever had to leave and, at the same time, to emphasize that this is the last thing you would ever want to do.

What you will accomplish by this is as follows:

- You will have told your employer that you've twigged the reasons why you're not getting the pay increases you deserve.
- You will have sent out a coded message that you *are* capable of going out and finding yourself another job, i.e. the big wide world doesn't frighten you.
- By saying you don't really want to leave, you will have pre-empted anyone taking your words as threats (threats invite negative responses, remember).

Will this work? In some cases, yes; in others, no. If it doesn't what we're moving onto next (internal networking) might provide the answers.

Internal networking

Internal networking is important for everyone. In other words, it's prick up your ears time because this is for you, whoever you are!

CASE STUDY: ROS, KAREN, DIANA AND JAN

Ros has been a key figure in Karen's section for some time. The problem, however, is that Karen is notoriously backward when it comes to putting forward her staff for salary increase. As a result, Karen's team is poorly paid compared to other parts of the company – a situation that has gone on for a number of years.

Fed up with what she feels is inadequate recognition for the effort she is putting in, Ros decides to have a word with Karen. She chooses to do this one night after work. The outcome of the meeting is, however, disappointing: Karen simply stonewalls, telling Ros she can see no reason for increasing her pay at this particular point in time. Afterwards Ros goes home feeling bitter and angry – hence the first thing she does when she gets back is to pick up the paper and start looking through the job ads.

This is typically where most people feel they've hit the brick wall and, like Ros, they react by seeing if the outside job market can offer them what they can't negotiate for themselves internally. But is there another path available to people like Ros? Let's return to the case study and find out.

CASE STUDY CONTINUED

Though Ros is a modest kind of person, what strikes her immediately as she scans through the job ads is that the company would be in real difficulties if she decided to leave. Her experience alone would be impossible to replace and they would be very hard pushed indeed to find anyone with her flair and feel for the job. Ironically, they would probably end up having to pay an inflated salary just to attract the right kind of applicant – stupid when, for the same money, they could keep her happy for years. At this juncture, a thought that occurs to Ros is to try going over Karen's head by speaking directly to Diana, the Chief Executive. Diana is no pushover but, being a good businesswoman, she will surely see the sense in keeping the talent in the company on board and not letting it drift off into the hands of the competition. What's bothering Ros, though, is if she's wrong in this assumption. If she goes over Karen's head and gets nowhere then she really will be in a difficult position.

Ros's reading of the situation is spot on, of course. Karen probably won't be very happy to find someone's gone behind her back – meaning she could react in a number of ways (none of them very helpful to Ros).

CASE STUDY CONTINUED

Because of the nature of her work, Ros has got a close association with Jan, the Company Accountant. Jan needs information from time to time on the costing of jobs and, because of her knowledge, Ros has always been the one to supply it. It is Jan who Ros goes to see the day after her meeting with Karen.

Jan is disturbed to hear Ros's tale of woe. In particular, she is disturbed that the problem of Ros's salary could not have been resolved by Karen – though she knows Karen of old, including how pig-headed she can be when it comes to dealing with staff. Jan has a high opinion of Ros. She is by far the most helpful person in Karen's team – always certain of her facts, always prepared to dig and delve in old files when more information is required, always courteous and well turned out. What a sad day it would be for the company if Ros ever decided to leave.

Later that day Jan has a meeting scheduled with Diana. When they finish talking about the business in hand, Jan raises the subject of Ros on the basis that it's something Diana needs to know about. Diana listens sympathetically. At first she blames herself for not keeping a more vigilant eye on the salaries in Karen's section (she too knows Karen of old). Like Jan, Diana also holds Ros in high regard and the last thing she wants is for her to leave – particularly if leaving means going to work for one of their many competitors (they would all be very keen to acquire someone with Ros's talents).

Sitting alone in her office afterwards, Diana reflects on what to do. Somehow she has to broach the subject of Ros's salary with Karen. Somehow she has to persuade Karen that Ros deserves an increase. Somehow too, she's got to let Karen feel it's her own decision. Diana sighs. Sometimes it's tough being a Chief Executive.

The points to pick out of this case study are as follows:

- Unintentionally perhaps, Ros got her pay rise by using her internal network. Through Jan she was able to get the ear of Diana without incurring the risks a direct approach would have involved.
- The networking worked because Jan held Ros in high regard (a spin-off from Ros's excellent use of Lifelong Interview skills, i.e. being helpful, courteous etc.).
- People like Ros (people with excellence on their side) can use internal networking to further their pay aims.
- The power of networking can come to the aid of people who find difficulty in bringing their silent bargaining power to bear, e.g. people who have become part of the furniture, people with boss problems, people like teleworkers who are remote from the seats of decision-making.

NOTEPAD

Networking is a subject all on its own. Suffice it to say that, in the context of career self-management, it is a very powerful tool indeed. A further example of its use in pay bargaining is in profiling companies from the point of view of being good providers. Some of the information you need can often be best sourced from internal network contacts.

Converting excellence into pay

Though pay structures vary enormously from one organization to the next, the extent to which they are formalized tends to depend on how many people are employed. Big employers, on the whole, have set scales for each given level of responsibility in the organization or bands within which individual salaries are fixed.

Smaller employers, on the other hand, can usually afford to be rather more ad hoc in their approach. An underlying question, however, in all bargaining where excellence is the issue, is what scope there is in the system for rewarding merit? At the worst extreme, there is a fixed salary for the job and that is that. Good and bad performers are paid alike. Pay structures decided by collective bargaining often fall into this category. Or else the bands for rewarding merit are narrow (often too narrow to be meaningful).

The point here is that no amount of silent bargaining power will help you to reap the rewards of excellence if your employer is constrained by rigid pay structures. It goes back to profiling your employer and doing this exercise as fully and properly as you can. If you do, it can save you much pain and disappointment later on. Where rigid pay structures are in force, the way forward is to use silent bargaining power generated by excellence to access promotion (in other words to move up to the next grade). This is a case of identifying aims that are *realizable* as distinct from those that are not.

Given, however, more flexible pay structures or graded pay structures that have substantial scope for rewarding merit, the way is open for you to bring your silent bargaining power to bear. A point to note here is that small companies and the loosely organized, semi-autonomous constituents of large fragmented groups are most susceptible to pay bargaining based on merit because:

- they are least likely to have rigid pay structures
- the loss of key people will have a more serious impact on them (simply because key people in these organizations are thinner on the ground).

Acquiring excellence

We put this in as a footnote to remind you that, rather like skills and experience, excellence is *acquirable* simply by putting in more effort. Again this is one of the spin offs from your Lifelong Interview. Get this right and a lot of other things will start to come together for you.

Questions and answers

Where performance is influenced by other factors

Q *Last year my sales were 70% up on the year before and, since I am paid a straight salary, I put it to my boss that I needed some recognition in the form of extra money in my pay packet. His response was that sales could just as easily nose-dive next year and my salary took account of these ups and downs. Whilst I understand what he is saying, do you have any advice on how I should proceed?*

A Your performance, we suspect, is based partly on your efforts and partly on market conditions, so your bumper year last year needs to be seen in this light, i.e. it wasn't entirely the result of your personal excellence. The real question, however, is what impact does last year's performance have on your silent bargaining power? Judging by your boss's reaction to your pay bid, the answer to the question appears to be 'very little' and this points to the market being the major factor in your high level of sales. Suggestions? A bonus perhaps (see Chapter 5), but don't fall into the trap of trading off part of your straight salary for a performance-related element when performance is largely subject to factors outside your control – furthermore factors which could prove to be volatile.

Loss of superannuation rights

Q *I suppose I come under the heading of being part of the furniture but one of my genuine concerns is that leaving my company will play havoc with my superannuation rights. How do you suggest I face up to this one?*

A Hold on, who said anything about leaving? Leaving or threatening to leave is the antithesis of silent bargaining power and if you are in any doubt about this read the relevant sections of Chapter 1 again. The object of the exercise you need to embark on is to dispel any impression your employer may have formed that you're welded to the fabric of the organization for good, i.e. the kind of impression that could lead to them taking you for granted and treating your pay ambitions dismissively as a result.

Golden handcuffs

Q *Are you saying that perks such as low interest loans and stock options have a detrimental effect on silent bargaining power? If so what is someone who is a recipient supposed to do about it?*

A Low interest loans and stock options are examples of golden handcuffs (retention devices used by employers to make it difficult for key people to contemplate leaving). Will they have a detrimental effect on your silent bargaining power? Yes, they will if they are seen to be working. The impression you must always create therefore is that, whilst you are fully appreciative of the perk, it would never stand in your way if it became right for you to make a move to another employer.

Networking – lack of trust

Q *I am in a very similar situation to Ros in your case study except I can think of no one internally with whom I would be happy to share my concerns about my pay. I think this simply boils down to a question of trust. Given the situation, do you agree I am right to hold back? If so, is there any other way networking can help me?*

A Yes you are right. Never network with anyone unless you have complete confidence in them. As to other ways in which networking can help you, do you know anyone outside your organization who would be able to put a word in the right ear for you? Professional advisers such as accountants, lawyers and management consultants may be able to fulfil this role.

Summary

Excellence (being the best) can convert directly into silent bargaining power, but only if your employer shares the same view of your excellence as you do. In some instances, what you take as an indication of recognition of your excellence is not what it seems (as in Qurban's case). In others, your excellence may not be transmitting itself to the right quarters, meaning your silent bargaining power has little or no effect. With the latter we have seen the importance of visibility (maintaining a high enough profile on the corporate scene to enable your talents to be appreciated). We have seen also how internal networking can provide the answers when articulating your excellence and bringing your silent bargaining to bear proves difficult (as in Ros's case).

Verdict on being the best

Good points

Improving performance improves promotion prospects as well as bringing pay rises.

Bad points

Excellence calls for a lot of effort which won't have any pay back if employers can't deliver. (This again emphasizes the importance of getting your profiling right).

4 | BEING PROMOTED

One way to get a pay rise is by getting yourself promoted to a position in which you are viewed as having more worth. You take the next step up the ladder and you get a pay rise as a result.

In this chapter we are going to look at:

- Whether your employer can provide you with the promotion opportunities you are seeking – where you could be pursuing ambitions that have little or no chance of ever being realized
- How to go about getting promotion – a step-by-step approach
- Politics – using conflicting interest groups in organizations to your advantage
- Overcoming obstacles in your path
- What to do when your promotion doesn't bring you the level of pay you expected
- Promotion for people who work in small firms and 'flat' organizations
- Promotion for people who work from home

Assessing your chances of promotion
Could your employer promote you?

The first question to ask yourself before setting off in pursuit of any kind of career aim is whether the aim is realizable – in this case, whether your employer can provide you with the kind of promotion opportunities you are seeking, i.e. ones that will give you more pay.

Clearly this is an important question to ask because if, for any reason, your employer is not able to provide you with the next step up the ladder, expending effort in this direction is utterly pointless. Here are three examples of people in situations where promotion could be difficult or impossible:

- **Garth** works for a small family business. Garth's bosses are all members of the family.
- **Kath**'s company took a layer out of its management structure 2 years ago, meaning Kath's avenues for promotion have effectively been taken away.
- **Jerome**'s division was hived off into a free standing business at the beginning of the year. Jerome, therefore, no longer has the opportunity to progress his career within a large international group.

These three examples typify the situations a lot of people find themselves in these days – specifically:

- More and more people work in small firms where access to the top echelons of management may be restricted to these who have a stake in the business, in the form of ownership of part of the equity.
- More and more companies have adopted 'flat' structures. The management pyramids on which people's careers were once based are no longer there.
- Large groups have divested themselves of parts they don't see as viable or which don't fit into their new visions of the future.
- New identities have sprung up from actions such as management buy-outs.

Sometimes the promotion opportunities aren't there for other reasons:

- **Darren**'s boss is 34, in good health and unlikely to leave.
- **Mo** works for a company where the best jobs always go to people they recruit from outside.
- **Daisy**'s firm is being slowly driven out of the market by global competition.

Again, this brings us back to the importance of profiling. In this instance, your profiling needs to establish how your employer measures up as a provider of promotion opportunities. The object of the exercise is to identify situations such as those above in which you could be setting off in pursuit of something that is unattainable from any practical standpoint.

Are you promotable?

The other factor in the advancement equation is you, of course. Are you ready to make that next giant leap forward in your career, or would you be viewed as over-reaching if you tried to put your name in the hat for promotion?

Needless to say, we are entering into the world of subjective judgements again. How you view yourself may be poles apart from how your employer views you, and this is something you must always allow for. Even where formal appraisal systems are in place, it is sometimes difficult to read your employer's innermost thoughts. The next subject we're going to look at, therefore, is communicating your ambitions – telling your boss that you are looking for promotion and the reasons why. One of the spin offs from entering into this kind of dialogue with the person you report to is that you should get some feedback. From the feedback you should be able to get some pretty strong clues as to whether you're seen as promotion material or not (more on this in a moment).

Communicating your ambitions

CASE STUDY: OLIVER AND TOM

Oliver is 28, ambitious and, in his own mind, ready to take on new challenges and responsibilities. Imagine, therefore, his disappointment when a vacancy for a Branch Manager was given to an outsider (someone who works for a competitor).

Incensed about what he sees as being passed over, Oliver asks to speak to his Divisional Director, Tom. He puts it to Tom that he wasn't given the opportunity to apply for the position. To his amazement, Tom replies by saying he didn't have any inkling

---

Oliver was the least bit interested in being a branch manager. Indeed, he suggests Oliver should blame himself for not making his ambitions more clear.

The real Oliver in this case study came away from the interview with his Director feeling pretty fed up with the way he'd been treated. Notably, he felt that internal candidates, such as himself, should have automatic preference when it comes to a promotion opportunity. In particular, he felt that he should not have been put in the position of having to 'say something' in order to get his face in the frame.

We can argue all day about the rights and wrongs of this situation but, sadly, people's ambitions do get misinterpreted and, if our experience is anything to go by, this happens quite a lot. The upshot, as here, is that some loyal, conscientious employee goes away feeling badly let down. It is usually the spark that sets them off on the road to looking for another job.

So what's the answer? Simply this: responsibility for managing your career, including making your ambitions known, rests firmly with you. Oliver, in other words, should have been transmitting appropriate messages upwards long before any of this happened and Tom should have been left in no doubt at all that Oliver wanted promotion. In short, there should be no room for misinterpretation with a matter as important as your future.

NOTEPAD

This is a further instance of bringing silent bargaining power to bear – this time to get promotion (and the pay rise that comes with it). Aware of Oliver's burning ambition, Tom would have realized for himself the dangers of appointing the new Branch Manager from outside and, if retaining Oliver in the business meant anything to him, he would have been at great pains to give him the first crack at the Branch Manager's job.

Communicating your ambitions doesn't have to be difficult and an occasion like an appraisal interview presents you with the perfect opportunity. For example, you may be asked how you see your future with the company unfolding – in which case you can spell it out to your audience in no uncertain terms. Where there is no appraisal system in place, you may have to find another occasion for making your ambitions known, but all that matters at the end of the day is that you are *understood*.

Listening to feedback

Communicating your ambitions properly has a further benefit. You can pick up some interesting feedback – feedback that tells you whether your boss views you as promotion material. Two tips for dealing with feedback are:

- Listen carefully to everything that is being said to you. In particular listen out for any suggestions that you may not be ready for promotion just yet, but that you could be with experience in x, y and z under your belt. Discussion should then proceed along the lines of how you are going to get x, y and z experience. For example, if you're seen as lacking in experience in dealing with disciplinary issues, could you get it either by (a) a secondment to the human resources department or (b) understudying someone who has to deal with a lot of disciplinary problems?

- Don't get drawn into arguments. If your boss is hostile to your ideas, leave it at that. A convenient exit line here is 'Perhaps we both need a little time to think it over.' Apart from anything else, this allows for the fact that your boss may simply be having a bad day, i.e. you had the bad luck to broach the subject of your ambitions at the wrong time.

A step-by-step approach to getting promotion

We have been trying to point out to you the benefits of adopting a structured or step-by-step approach to getting promotion. As discussed, the three steps are:

1 profiling (deciding whether the opportunities are there or not)

2 communicating (getting the message across)

3 listening (finding out how your employer views you).

By following this model you will:

- eliminate the pursuit of hard to achieve ambitions if it will be years before the opportunities you are seeking present themselves

- bring to bear any silent bargaining power you may have (your employer knows you want promotion, *ipso facto* your employer knows what might happen if you don't get it)

- know what stands in the way of you and promotion (if anything).

Having found out what stands in your way of promotion, you may decide to put your ambitions on hold until you have gained whatever experience you are seen as lacking in.

⚠ **WARNING!**

Promotion opportunities don't come up overnight. Even if your employer is waving the green flag at you, it could still be years before the right opening presents itself. You may not be prepared to wait for years, of course.

Politics

Politics – the interplay of rival factions in businesses – can have a great bearing on whether you are promoted or not. A further case study helps to illustrate how this can happen.

CASE STUDY: JAMIE, PETER, THOMAS AND ESTELLE

The company is about to make a new senior appointment – a General Manager to take charge of a recently acquired business into which significant sums of money are going to be ploughed. Jamie, the Sales and Marketing Director, is pressing for Peter one of his assistants to get the new job, whilst Thomas, the Production Director, wants it to go to Estelle, a bright young engineer who works in his team. Conversely, Thomas sees Peter as being in Jamie's pocket and Jamie has much the same view of Estelle. With their respective candidates in mind, both Thomas and Jamie are doing their best to bend the Chief Executive's ear.

Reading between the lines, this sounds like the sort of sales versus production rivalry that is found in many manufacturing companies – rivalry that often centres round the two leading figures in each faction, in this case Jamie and Thomas. With the appointment of the new General Manager, who gets the job depends on which Director has the most influence with the Chief Executive. If it is Jamie, then Peter will be favourite. If it is Thomas, then Estelle will clearly be in pole position.

The point to note about politics is that you're more likely to encounter them the higher up the ladder you're seeking to reach. There is far more at stake with top jobs and competing factions may try to block your path forward because they view you as a threat to their own interests.

Half the battle with politics is accepting that they're there, i.e. accepting that some of the faces you meet on your journey up the corporate ladder will be well disposed towards you whilst others won't. Given this acceptance, you can start to form an appreciation of what it will take to smooth the way forward. To do this:

■ Take an entirely practical view of politics – where can you use them to help? Where could they pose problems for you? Anticipate what the problems are likely to be and try to deal with them.

- Identify your supporters – who in the organization will back you in your bid for promotion? Often these will be people whose patronage you have enjoyed in the past; people who have been there before to give you a helping hand.

- Similarly, identify where the opposition is likely to come from – who could see your progress in the organization as a threat?

- Talk to your supporters and voice your concerns about any opposition – see what suggestions they have.

- Use your supporters to give weight to your campaign – particularly where your supporters have access to the ears of those who can influence the outcomes you are seeking.

NOTEPAD

We're seeing again the benefits to be had from internal networking – in this instance from networking with people who (a) can support you in your bid from promotion and (b) can help you to fight off opposition.

If you have powerful voices behind you in your bid for promotion, how can use them to overcome opposition? What is the range of options open to you? The next case study might help you to see some of the possibilities.

CASE STUDY: RICKY, FOSTER AND ANIL

Ricky is in line for promotion to the Board of Management but he realizes that, while some voices on the Board will be speaking in his favour, others won't. Chief among Ricky's supporters is his old boss, Foster. Foster was Ricky's original role model when he joined the company 10 years ago and Foster has been behind all his moves upwards so far. The opposition camp is led by Anil. Anil views Ricky as Foster's yes man – someone who will go with Foster on all issues, hence a potential threat to his own position. Ricky knows that Anil can be very persuasive and how other Board members could easily be swayed by his arguments.

Ricky voices these concerns to Foster. Foster thinks for a few minutes then comes up with his own idea. He'll tell Anil that, in exchange for dropping his opposition to Ricky's promotion he'll give his full support to one of Anil's pet schemes. Anil won't be able to resist this offer, he feels.

Equating promotion to tangible gains in earnings

Fundamental to striving to get promoted is the outcome: you want to see benefits for taking on extra responsibilities – results in the shape of more money.

How much more is, of course, difficult for you to quantify. In organizations where pay is graded into published bands, you will know exactly what to expect from your promotion in money terms. In less stratified organizations, you are left having to make your own assessment of what level of salary increase your promotion deserves. In some instances, you may be pleasantly surprised by your employer's largesse but in others you could find yourself bitterly disappointed to the point at which you wonder whether all the effort it took to get yourself promoted was really worth it. Finding that promotion doesn't yield quite the gains you expected is the subject we want to take a look at next. Once again, a short case study will help to bring out the important points.

CASE STUDY: ANGIE

Following the promotion of her boss, Ralph, Angie has been put in charge of the department – an ambition she has cherished for many years. Imagine her disappointment, therefore, when she receives her appointment letter from the Chief Executive detailing her new salary and indicating a figure way below her expectations. Angie is so upset that, at first, she is tempted to go and tell the Chief Executive what to do with the job. In the end, however, caution wins the day and she bites her tongue. She is still far from happy, though. Ralph never discussed his salary with her, but she is sure he earned far more for shouldering exactly the same responsibilities as the ones she is being asked to take on. In her view this isn't fair.

Part of Angie's problem is she feels slighted, illustrating an important point about pay – it's not just the money and what it buys. It's also the way in which we feel we're being recognized. Feeling underpaid inevitably brings a feeling of being under appreciated, and this is something that saps our self-confidence and influences the way we feel about our work.

But back to Angie. Having decided very sensibly not to tell the Chief Executive to stick his new job, what should she do next?

The first question she has to ask herself is what the expectation of her earnings after promotion was based on. Was it a rough guess at what the previous incumbent, Ralph, was getting (as seems to be the case) or was she comparing herself with others in similar positions? Or was it that the increase simply didn't seem to be big enough, i.e. the differential between what she earned previously and her new salary didn't somehow seem to reflect the added responsibilities?

Comparators

Except in the case of graded pay structures (where you can check out easily whether you're being paid the right salary for the job) finding internal benchmarks on which to base judgements about your pay is notoriously difficult. There are two main reasons for saying this:

1 Picking comparators is largely subjective, i.e. you and your employer may have very different views as to who is comparable in terms of job responsibilities.

2 You may not actually know how much your comparators are paid (salary information may not be something you share with your peers).

The bottom line to this little homily about comparators is to urge you to be cautious. Wading in with statements like 'I'm not paid as much as so-and-so' can be doubly dangerous:

■ You may be wrong.

■ You may not know all the relevant circumstances. For example, the person with whom you're comparing yourself could be someone your employer views as an anomaly (all organizations have anomalies). In short, if you were to cast your net a little wider and sample a lot more people across the organization, you might find that a different picture emerges (possibly one which shows you as highly paid compared with others in your peer group!).

Furthermore, because you're newly promoted, your employer may want to see how you get on with your new responsibilities before offering a big pay rise. In Angie's case, Ralph her predecessor, had presumably been in the job for some time, so his salary reflected considerable experience. The fact that he's been promoted is also an indicator that he's done the job well, meaning his salary probably includes elements that take account of his previous performance. Angie, of course, qualifies on neither of these scores – at least, not yet.

Negotiating a deal to reflect responsibility

Pursuing goals in an organization is a lot easier if you take your aims one at a time. With promotion, achieving the aim (getting promoted) usually means you achieve a second aim as well (getting the appropriate pay rise). However, if you don't achieve the second aim (the pay rise is measly), you need to go back to separating your aims out.

What this means in practice is this:

■ Start by biting your tongue (as Angie did). Jumping in with a bid for more pay on day one in a new job is hardly likely to do you much good and, in any case, will probably invite a negative response.

■ Give the new job your absolute best shot. Show that, in picking you, your employer made the right choice.

■ Leave it, say, 6 months, then broach the subject of your pay. You will then have the silent bargaining power that comes with your increased responsibilities and a successful 6-month track record.

■ Proceed in the same way as set out in Chapter 1.

Promotion for people who work in small firms and 'flat' organizations

We have included this section for two reasons:

1 More and more people work in small firms or in organizations where levels of management have been stripped out (usually for cost saving reasons).

2 People in small firms and flat organizations tend to see their promotion channels as blocked or severely restricted.

Here is an example of a real-life problem faced, from time to time by people working in small firms and flat organizations:

CASE STUDY: CLINT

Clint works for a company in the chemical industry. When he first joined the firm 7 years ago, his promotion path was clearly mapped out. From his present position of Team Leader, he could aspire to any one of a number of middle management jobs, before moving on to take charge of a site – a move which would bring him an automatic seat on the company's Board of Management.

Five years ago, however, Clint's company hit hard times. Instructions came down from Head Office to reduce overheads – or else – and this culminated in a massive shake out. Among those to go was the entire middle management stratum – some of whom opted for redundancy, while others were assimilated into other roles around the group. This delayering left Clint and the

> other 20 team leaders reporting directly to the Manager in charge of the site. With the middle management grade now gone, Clint views his chances of promotion as practically nil. Besides, if the site manager's job did become vacant, at least five of the other team leaders have more experience than he has.

People in Clint's position usually end up seeking to fulfil their ambitions by putting themselves on the outside job market to see what opportunities for upward mobility other employers can offer them (i.e. incurring the risks that go with changing employers – a subject we will be coming back to in Chapter 7). But the reality of flat organizations is that they are not quite so bereft of opportunities as they first seem.

Opportunities in flat organizations

Although sweeping changes always accompany the stripping out of levels of management, the jobs previously done by the tier now missing don't simply go away. They're assimilated either upwards or downwards, meaning, in Clint's case, that some of the jobs previously done by the middle management grade will now be done by the site manager and that others will come down to Clint's team leader level. Straight away, therefore, Clint has acquired more power to his elbow, in the way of silent bargaining power, than he thinks. But the story doesn't stop there. With more responsibilities and 20 team leaders now reporting to him, the Site Manager has far more than he can handle. Hence, any opportunities for offloading jobs will tend to be grasped eagerly. It's back to those magic words again: 'I can do that – leave it to me.' The knock-on effect is, of course, enhancement of silent bargaining power. Clint has, in effect, promoted himself in all but name and he can now move on to converting the added responsibilities he has acquired into hard cash. Clint's chances? Pretty good we would say. The very last thing his poor, overstretched Site Manager would want is for Clint to up and leave (the newly delegated responsibilities would be on their way straight back into his hands!).

A similar situation exists in small companies where pairs of hands are thin on the ground and where busy people at the top are usually more than willing to delegate responsibilities downwards.

NOTEPAD

Taking on more responsibility has the double advantage of adding to your skills and broadening your experience. In short, your silent bargaining power receives a massive boost which you will be able to use to your advantage in the fullness of time.

⚠ **WARNING!**

To harp on a point we've made previously, don't expect the offer of money to be made up front in these situations. Sometimes it will but, if it doesn't happen, don't let it get in the way. This is your opportunity to acquire a big injection of silent bargaining power. The pay off comes later, don't forget.

Promotion for people who work from home

People who work from home also have problems when it comes to promotion.

CASE STUDY: PETRA

Petra sells insurance to a specialist market and she works from home, servicing clients within a 50-mile radius of where she lives. Petra likes working from home. It enables her to spend more time with her family and she doesn't have to face the grind of travelling into an office through the rush-hour traffic every day (an aspect of her last job that she hated). Indeed most of what she does, she finds she can do over the phone anyway. On average she is only spending a day and a half a week out visiting clients.

A recent development, however, has put Petra in a bit of a dilemma. The National Sales Manager rang her up the other day to ask her if she would be interested in taking on a new role in the company. The job and the package were both very interesting but what has given rise to the conflict in Petra's mind is the fact that it is based in head office 80 miles away. Whilst the company has said it would not expect her to relocate, the idea of commuting daily over that kind of distance is not one that appeals to Petra in the slightest. She won't have the flexibility she currently enjoys to run work in tandem with her family life. Neither is she so sure she wants to work in an office with other people again.

Petra's case study illustrates that people who work from home usually do so for a reason. Either they enjoy the ambience, the fact that they can fit work around their domestic routines appeals to them, or they may simply like the greater freedom. Indeed, all three factors may be important. Promotion can, of course, mean having to be office based and this isn't necessarily consistent with what the Petras of this world want out of life. In short, if you currently work from home, ask yourself *before* you go for promotion:

- What would you do if the promotion would mean you could no longer work from home?
- If so, is this something you really want?

Having thought through these questions and decided that you are happy to go ahead with your quest for promotion, your first task is to make sure you don't get overlooked simply because your face is not in evidence every day (as it would be if you were office-based). 'Out of sight – out of mind' is the reason why a lot of people who work from home get passed over when it comes to promotion and you need to make sure this doesn't happen to you. The bottom line here is ensuring that the people you work for understand exactly what your aspirations are (back to the business of communicating your aims properly again). Also, let them know that just because you're home-based now doesn't mean you're permanently attached to the idea. We say this because, with home-based people, a frequent source of misunderstanding arises from employers *assuming* that this is the way they wish to carry on. So a statement to the contrary needs to come from you.

Questions and answers

Passed over

Q *I have recently suffered the disappointment of seeing what would have been a good promotion opportunity for me filled by an outsider (someone from my Divisional Manager's old firm). What do I do next? Clearly complaining about what's happened won't get me anywhere.*

A Complaining no – but what you do need to do is ask yourself whether your Divisional Manager *knew* of your interest in the job or not. In other words, had you *communicated* your ambition sufficiently? If the answer to this question is no, then clearly what you need to do next is go knocking on his or her door. If the answer is yes, then you must read this passing over as a bad sign. Either your boss has a preference for old pals or they don't rate the internal talent – it hardly matters which because the result is just the same as far as you are concerned. What to do in these situations? Wait and see what happens next time a promotion opportunity comes up but don't wait any longer than that. It could be the signal to you that the time has come to start shopping in the outside job market.

Not ready for promotion

Q *I applied for an Area Manager's job advertised internally on notice boards but I was told at the interview that I couldn't be considered because I lacked experience on our full range of products. Whilst accepting that an Area Manager's product knowledge needs to be flawless, I do however feel that the gaps in*

*my experience were ones that could be filled fairly easily (for
example, by seconding me to a couple of other departments for
short periods). I made this point at the interview because I wanted
to feel that I could apply for any area managers' jobs that came up
in the future. The reaction I got, though, was quite surprising.
Seconding me to other departments seemed to present all sorts of
difficulties and my suggestion was turned down flat. My problem
now is that I don't see how I'm going to get the experience I need to
get promotion. In short, I seem to be in a Catch 22 situation. Where
do I go from here?*

A Sometimes telling people they haven't got enough experience is
a way of fobbing them off and we wonder if this is what has
happened to you. Your employer's reluctance to give you the
experience you need certainly seems to point to them having other
reservations about your suitability – reservations they don't feel
comfortable about discussing with you. Advice? Speak to your
bosses again and put it to them that you're ambitious, meaning
you're anxious to find a way of overcoming your lack of
experience. If your idea of secondment is out of the question, then
do they have any suggestion on what to do? This time watch their
lips carefully. Any further prevarication should be read as a sign
that they have 'other reasons' for not seeing you as suitable
promotion material. View this as evidence that what you are
attempting to do is not realizable.

Promised promotion that never comes

Q *I made a case for promotion 3 years ago and my boss agreed
that it was right for me to be having ambitions to move up the tree.
Since then very little has happened. Every time I broach the subject
the answer I get back is 'wait and see'. My question is how long do
I wait?' I am 36 next birthday and I feel that some of my best years
for getting promotion are slipping away from me.*

A Don't panic yet, but you are right in your general appreciation of
the situation. The years between 25 and 40 are important ones for
making major advances in your career (and in your earnings) and,
as far as your employer is concerned, it could be that they're not
really able to provide you with the opportunities you are seeking
(employers sometimes delude themselves in these matters).

Equally (and more sinisterly), they could feel they have something to gain by stringing you along with half promises (thereby retaining you in the business for as long as possible). How long do you wait? Accepting that it's intrinsically difficult to lay down time periods for employers to come up with promotion opportunities, it is equally important to accept that, from your point of view, the period can't go on being open-ended. Our suggestion, therefore, is this: put a deadline on getting promoted (say 12 months hence) and mark this date on your calendar as the date when you start getting off some job applications. The deadline, by the way, is for your own reference only (i.e. not for onward transmission to your employer, which could be construed as the kind of threat that invites a negative response). Also, just in case it's been some time since you last gave them a reminder about your aspirations, a further discussion with them would probably do no harm.

Promotion has meant I am earning less

Q *I was promoted to a management job this summer only to find that I no longer qualify for overtime payments, meaning I am now earning less than I earned previously. What's the answer here?*

A It's not clear how you got yourself into this situation. Presumably you knew that managers didn't qualify for overtime payments when you took the job, so this was a factor you took into account, i.e. you saw the promotion more for the opportunities it would access for you in the future than for its earnings potential now. Occasionally, people put in situations like yours 'retaliate' by going off on the dot every night – leaving some of their newly acquired management responsibilities undischarged in the process. Clearly you will achieve little from doing this – other than a worthless feeling of self-satisfaction. Furthermore, you could be putting yourself at risk. Our advice? Bide your time until you feel comfortable that you're doing the job to everyone's satisfaction, then raise the subject of your pay. At this point you will have more in the way of silent bargaining power on your side.

Staying out of politics

Q *Surely the best advice to give about politics is to stay out of them. Why don't you say this?*

A Because in practice it can be difficult to achieve. The path you take upwards in organizations, the people you work for, the policies you back all serve to determine which camp you belong to in the eyes of others and whether you agree or not won't come into it. Hence our advice with politics is to accept them for what they are, learn to live with them and play them to your advantage as and when opportunities arise.

Rise following promotion payable in instalments

Q *The rise I get following my promotion is payable in two instalments – part now and the bigger part in six months' time. Whilst I don't intend to quibble about this, it still rankles slightly because I am taking on a lot more responsibility – including a backlog of work from my predecessor. What do you say?*

A Your employer clearly wants to see how you perform in the job before paying you the bulk of the increase and this seems reasonable enough to us. So, no, don't queer the pitch by quibbling. Instead get stuck in. Give your new responsibilities your best shot. Clear up the backlog and prove to your employers that they've made the right choice.

Summary

Pay isn't usually the *only* driving force behind going for promotion. Most of us do it for other reasons – like seeking to achieve the career goals we have set for ourselves. More pay is simply the spin-off, the reward we pick up as we make our way along our upwardly spiralling path.

Going after promotion is, therefore, something you need to see in the round, not just as a means of pursing narrowly defined objectives like pay. For a start, promotion will bring bigger responsibilities and this is something you need to feel completely confident about. Put simply, the worst scenario of all is finding yourself in a job where you are totally out of your depth. Yes, the exit routes are there, but they're all pretty painful.

Similarly, in your anxiety to get promotion and the better pay that goes with it, you could overlook how it might affect your life. In this chapter for instance, we talked about people who work from home, perhaps people who are very happy to be sitting out in the garden on a nice sunny day with their lap tops and mobile phones, people who wouldn't necessarily find it that easy to fit into office life, people for whom elevation to higher rank could, therefore, spell out misery in one form or another.

Key point

Promotion must be seen in its wider context. Go for it only when it's right for you. By the same token, know when it's best left well alone. Certainly, never let the lure of riches dazzle you (the riches in such cases could prove to be very short term).

Given promotion is an avenue you wish to pursue, you need to satisfy yourself first of all that your employer can provide the opportunities you are seeking and that, by expending effort in this direction, you won't be banging your head on a big brick wall. Because promotion is such a long-term business, people can end up spending years pursuing career objectives that, on closer inspection, were never attainable in the first place. Time is precious. Don't ever squander it.

Having established that the opportunities for promotion are there, use a structured (step-by-step) approach to achieving the aim you have set yourself. This means:

- **Communicate** your ideas – make sure everyone knows where you're coming from. Remind them from time to time.

- **Listen** to any feedback, notably feedback that might indicate that (a) your bid for promotion has fallen on deaf ears or (b) you need more experience.

- **Act** on the feedback – if the shutters have gone up in your face, read this to mean that your aim wasn't realizable (i.e. your assessment of your employer was wrong). Where your experience appears to be the problem, take steps to remedy it.

Verdict on being promoted

Good points

Promotion is a natural extension to adding value to yourself and it could be the only way forward pay-wise in organizations where salaries are fixed to scales or grades. It also paves the way for further pay rises in future (as you climb even higher up the ladder).

Bad points

Promotion is unlikely to be achievable immediately. In some cases, it will take a very long time indeed. For this reason it may not be an acceptable option for those with pay problems that are pressing.

5 | GOING ONTO BONUS

One way of accessing higher earnings is by restructuring your pay package to include a bonus or performance-related element so that, if you're as good as you say you are, the performance-related part will reflect this fact. At least that's the theory. But in practice, how do you go about negotiating a performance-related pay package for yourself? What are the snags and how can you make the most out of flexible earnings? The topics we're going to look at in this chapter are:

- Is it for you? The pros and cons of performance-based pay
- The importance of making the right choice for yourself – applying the test of ultimate control
- How to negotiate a flexible earnings package – keeping your escape routes open
- Reviewing bonus arrangements – the importance of keeping them relevant to your circumstances

Knowing where you're coming from

Most performance-related pay novices approach the subject from the point of view of being straight salary earners. In some cases, these straight salaries may be supplemented by variable elements linked to profit, added value or some other measure of corporate performance. Nearly always in these cases, though, the variable element is small in relation to the total package and it is paid across the board to a number of people, i.e. not targeted to specific individuals.

The point to this short discourse is to highlight, that for many people, going onto performance-related pay is a new experience. They're entering unknown territory; they're wary and quite rightly so. Indeed 'Is this for me?' is a question they are right to be asking themselves.

Outside manual occupations, people employed in direct sales are most commonly paid bonuses and commissions based on individual performance. Converting a customer's enquiry into an order is more or less a direct measure of the salesman's skill – or so it seems. Similarly, the number of orders processed in total may be seen to equate roughly to the effort the salesman puts in. The sales value generated by each specific individual seems, therefore, a pretty accurate measure of performance and the bonus or commission paid acts as both a reward and an incentive (to go on pulling in the orders).

Not everyone, though, carries out a function which has some easily measurable output. For instance, how do you measure the performance of a Human Resources Manager? On the number of days saved by prompt resolution of industrial disputes perhaps? Or could this lead to a capitulatory approach when dealing with organized labour (something not necessarily in the company's best interests)? All this serves to illustrate why employers are also wary of performance-related pay. Often they're the ones saying 'Is this for me?' – a point to take into account when entering into negotiations on bonuses.

Fully Flexible Finances (FFF)

This is a book about getting a better deal for yourself pay-wise. Our interest in bonuses is, therefore, slanted towards the extent to which they can help you to achieve this objective. This brings us to the first and most fundamental point about performance-related packages – they can go up and they can go down and this, in itself, can be very difficult to live with.

CASE STUDY: AL

Al is in charge of a small, specialist division of a large company in the telecommunications industry. Three years ago Al negotiated a bonus for himself based on the division's profitability. In the first year this bonus yielded 25% on top of his earnings. Year two was even better with bonus earnings equating to roughly 40% of his basic pay. On the strength of these results, Al made the decision to buy a bigger property for his family. He also sent his two children to more expensive schools and, at the same time, he and his wife joined an exclusive golf club.

Then the problems started. Last year's profits were affected by adverse trading conditions. In addition to which, an unforeseen global shortage of key components sent their price sky high. The knock-on effect was to wipe out the division's profits almost overnight, meaning Al's bonus package paid out nothing last year. The picture for next year doesn't look any rosier either and Al is now worried about keeping up with the payments on the house. As for school fees, he is seeing what cut-backs he can make in other areas so he can go on paying them and avoid disrupting the children's education. Membership of the golf club is certainly something he can no longer afford.

The object lesson here is not to introduce overheads into your life which you can only pay for out of earnings which are subject to fluctuations. The temptation is sometimes hard to resist – particularly when the earnings have been good, historically speaking. It is very easy to get lulled into thinking that their (good) contribution will go on for ever.

This brings us to the subject of **Fully Flexible Finances** (FFF): having the capacity to shift outgoings upwards and downwards in line with incomings. Fully Flexible Finances originally came about in response to the modern career situation in which general instability and the need occasionally to combine income from several different sources meant that people could no longer rely on earnings that automatically went up year on year. The capacity to sideshift and downshift is fundamental to survival in today's world. Similarly, with earnings that go up and down, the secret of success is learning how to live with the variability.

Needless to say, some of your outgoings won't respond to this kind of treatment: for example, mortgage repayments and utilities bills. These are the core items of expenditure which your income always has to cover. Outside these core items, however, a surprising amount of scope is available to you (some companies even offer flexible mortgage packages – this might be a facility you want to consider). The following list of bullet points will help to give you some pointers:

- If you plan to go onto bonus, condition yourself to the idea of earnings that go up and down. Most importantly, accept that there will be good times and bad times. Allow for both.

- Separate out core and non-core items in your outgoings. Identify items where your spending could be tailored to what you can afford.

- See, for example, items like holidays as something you can spend more or less on – depending on the circumstances. View this as part of the fun.

- Don't notch up your overheads on the basis of what your bonus earnings yield in good years (as Al did). Finding you have to do without things you have become accustomed to will be very hard.

- Try to set aside some of the money you make in good years. Accumulate a war chest to see you through the bad times.

- Don't get thrown into despondency when you hit a bad patch. Just like good times, bad patches don't last for ever.

- Learn to look at bigger pictures. Don't view your earnings in one year as indicative of anything in particular. Base your opinions on longer periods of time.

■ Give yourself a treat whenever your bonus plan yields bumper earnings (this is important). By treat, we mean something like a nice holiday or some other one-off expenditure, as opposed to adding more and more items onto your overheads.

NOTEPAD

Accepting the idea of flexible finances is important if you are going to make a success out of performance-related pay. Equally, it's important that people who are dependent on you, such as your family, get the same message. Everyone needs to be attuned to FFF or life could prove very difficult indeed for you.

Preparing a case

Picking the right measure of performance

It will help at this point to define the task you are about to embark on. You are going to have to convince your employer to introduce a performance-related element into your pay and your employer isn't necessarily going to be too happy about the idea. But before you start getting locked into any discussions, you need to reflect for a while on what exactly you are going to propose. Notably you need to clarify in your own head what performance measures you are going to suggest.

Going back to Al for a moment, the performance measure in his case was the profit his division made but, whilst Al may be the man in charge, not all the factors that impact on profit are under his control. The reason his bonus earnings took such a nose dive was because of trading conditions and component shortages in the industry. He could do nothing about either except hope that better times would return soon.

The test of ultimate control

Picking the right performance measures is clearly very important to you and this is where you need to apply the 'test of ultimate control'. Put simply, you must ask yourself who, what or what combination of factors ultimately controls a particular standard of performance? Is it solely down to you, or do factors outside your control also have an impact? Obviously, the more factors under your control, the better it is for you. The less likely it is that something will come along out of the blue and wipe out your bonus earnings overnight – as happened in Al's case.

Is the idea sellable?

This brings us onto the next consideration. Is what you are proposing something your employer is going to buy, bearing in mind that they may be suspicious of what you're up to and will be looking for the catches.

Take a hypothetical example. You're proposing a bonus based on the number of cups of coffee you drink in a day; yes, it is within your control; but, no, your employer is hardly likely to be impressed by the idea. Even if you cut your coffee intake by 80% the reduced number of trips you make to the coffee machine is unlikely to have that great an impact on the business's performance. Your employer won't see any great reason for making the change, because, from their point of view, there are no tangible gains to be had. As a consequence, the likelihood is they will simply play safe and say no.

The lesson to take away from this rather silly example is that what passes the test of ultimate control with flying colours won't necessarily be very sellable when it comes to convincing your employer. In short, accept that you will have to make a few compromises.

Assessing the risk

Except in the case of quite basic occupations, you will find it very difficult indeed to devise any kind of bonus arrangement where the factors that affect performance are all under your control. This, however, is not really the object of the exercise. Applying the test of ultimate control just helps you to form a proper appreciation of the risk – in this case, the risk of basing part of your salary on a measure of performance.

A few general words about risk first of all. Risk is inherent in all situations in which you stand to gain something. Most of you will have got the message a long time ago that, if you don't take risks, you don't get very far in life.

Risk has always got two sides to it, an upside and a downside. In the case of performance-related pay, the upside is what you can gain from the arrangement (the extra money you can make). The downside is when the bonus yields nothing.

What's important about risk is that you face up to it. This means that:

■ You see where the risk could come from (by applying the test of ultimate control).

■ You look at both the upsides and the downsides, and form a balanced view.

■ With the downsides, you must consider the consequences. Would a 'worst case scenario' be catastrophic for you, or would you be able to limit the damage in some way (by applying FFF, for example)?

Getting your ideas together

To help you select the right performance-related pay arrangements for your situation, what we have looked at so far is:

■ the importance of picking the right performance measure (one where you will have at least some direct influence over what happens)

■ the realities of steering the idea past your employer

■ the different outlook that has to go with flexible earnings (the art of living with the highs and lows)

■ a proper appreciation of risk.

Let's move on now to pulling your ideas together. This is the preamble to commencing discussions with your employer. In other words, this is where we need to shape your ideas into a sellable form.

Selecting the right package

Broadly speaking, there are two options for performance-related pay:

1 **a lying-on-top arrangement** in which the performance-related element is simply added on to the existing salary. In terms of risk, it doesn't carry any downsides but, for obvious reasons, it could give you the biggest problems when it comes to getting your employer's approval (the gains all seem to go one way).

2 **a slice-for-slice arrangement** in which you forgo part of your existing salary in exchange for a performance-related element. Slice-for-slice is obviously more risky but, for reasons we will touch on shortly, it will probably be more acceptable to your employer.

Which one do you choose?

The answer is down to you and your attitude to risk. This is not just to do with the kind of person you are. Your personal circumstances also come into it. For instance, if you are young, single, foot-loose and fancy-free with no significant outgoings, other than keeping yourself in the manner to which you have become accustomed, your capacity to take risks is enormous. On the other hand, if you are mortgaged up to your eyeballs with a family to support, then taking big risks probably isn't for you. Don't, however, rule out the 'slice-for-slice' approach altogether because the risk factor clearly relates to the size of the slice.

Keep it simple

This is important. Over-complicating performance-related bonuses is a mistake and a reason why a lot of them go wrong. Here are some tips on keeping it simple:

■ Go for a measure of performance where the information is readily accessible, e.g. sales figures, profit or return on capital employed (all types of information that the system already pumps out).

Conversely, avoid measures where the information will need to be collated specially, or where a separate record keeping system would have to be set up.

■ Again, when picking a measure of performance, go for something where the end figure isn't subject to too many tamperings. Take profit for example. In some organizations, the profit of individual divisions or profit centres is subject to all sorts of adjustments, e.g. the allocation of charges for services provided by head office departments etc. Where bonuses are at stake, this could be a source of endless future arguments.

■ Avoid too many rules. Any problems are best sorted out with your employer as you go along. Proceed on the basis of mutual trust. This is better than pages and pages of small print, which tries to address every hypothetical situation (you won't think of all of them anyway).

■ Don't call in the management consultants. You could end up with something very complicated (something no one understands – including you).

Keep your escape routes open

Bonuses don't always work out in the way you think they're going to. This is why it is important to keep some escape routes open. Do this by:

■ introducing the bonus for a trial period at the start (say, 6 months). If it works out, fine; if it doesn't then you have the facility to ditch it early in its life (most bugs will appear in the first 6 months).

■ having periodic review dates thereafter (e.g. at the end of every year).

NOTEPAD

You could find that your employers are very wary when it comes to discussions about bonuses (a subject we will be looking at next). The provision of escape routes should help to overcome some their reservations. Your employers will see they have ways out too.

Anticipating your employer's reaction

Let's face it, someone asking to be put on a bonus is not an everyday event. Your employers may wonder what your game is. Their initial reaction may be to dig in their heels and to simply play safe.

Employers' concerns usually fall into two categories:

1 They're not too sure exactly what they're letting themselves in for (fear of the unknown).

2 There is the prospect with any bonus arrangement that it could spin out of control, meaning employers have to pay out huge sums for little or nothing in return.

Employers' attitudes are often conditioned by experiences and with bonuses, sadly, the experiences have not always been good. Anticipating a certain amount of opposition is, therefore, sensible. The challenge is for you to overcome these concerns.

Of course you are less likely to meet resistance if bonuses are the norm in your organization. If, for example, the Chief Executive is paid a bonus based on earnings per share, it is less likely to be a shock to the system that someone lower down the ladder also wants to be put on a bonus plan.

Here is where a little digging round can help you to form a view of the task ahead. Use this mini checklist to help you.

- Does your organization have an incentives culture?
- Is it common to find salary packages that contain performance-related elements?
- In particular, is it the norm for executive staff to be paid bonuses?

If you are able to answer yes to these questions, your suggestion that you go onto bonus shouldn't raise too many eyebrows. On the other hand, if incentive plans are practically unknown in your organization, then the path that lies ahead could be a difficult one.

Making a case for performance-related pay

Irrespective of whether you anticipate resistance or not, you will still have to put forward a good case. In this particular instance the case will rest on the reasons why you see a performance-related pay element as beneficial – both to you *and* to your employers. This mutuality of interest is important. They will be less likely to buy the idea if they think the gains are all going one way. Convincing arguments can be constructed around these issues:

- **Incentive** – it is important from both parties' points of view that you have the correct incentives, i.e. that your pay reflects how hard you work at getting sales, making more profits, maximizing the return on the assets you manage or whatever the proposed measure of your performance happens to be.

- **Reward** – it is equally important to both parties that you feel your effort is being recognized. Your continuing happiness is a matter of mutual concern.

- **Sharing the risk** – where you're proposing a 'slice-for-slice' arrangement, the fact that you're happy to take the downsides as well as the upsides should impress your employers. They will see this as splitting the risks both ways (you don't always come out the winner, so it's fair play).

■ **Integrity** – where resistance is anticipated, it might help to pre-empt it by making a statement to the effect that you've got no hidden agendas. Your reasons for wanting to go onto bonus are entirely as stated, and are above board.

■ **Let-outs** – as we've mentioned already, it will comfort your employers to know they have some escape routes. You are proposing a trial period and reviews at stated intervals after that. Both parties will have the option to pull out.

⚠ WARNING!

Some employers take the view that people in positions of responsibility shouldn't need incentives – giving your best at all times is something that is *expected* of you and is divorced from any considerations of monetary gain. Arguing your case on the need for incentives is hardly likely to carry much weight with employers such as these, so don't even attempt it.

What next?

Having made your case, the ball is now in your employer's court. What you are relying on is that:

■ you have made a convincing case

■ your silent bargaining power is working for you.

Your employer will have grasped the point that, even if you have not said so, you are not happy with things as they stand. The ramifications of saying no will, therefore, figure prominently in their minds.

Staying flexible

CASE STUDY: STUART

Stuart was appointed to head up a new business venture – a sales outlet that his company had set up in another part of the country. Previously, Stuart worked in a head office advisory role.

A few months into the new job, Stuart spotted the enormous potential for developing sales but, in his opinion, exploiting this potential called for a different and more entrepreneurial approach.

Consistent with this need, Stuart proposed to head office that part of his salary should be linked to profit. In his view, this would give him the incentive to roll up his sleeves and get more business, in the same way that the proprietor of a small firm would.

His bosses came back to him with a different idea, however. They told him they were not entirely comfortable with an entrepreneurial approach. They felt it could clash with the main objective of the new venture, which was to establish a long-term presence in the territory rather than go for fast growth. They proposed, therefore, that Stuart should have a bonus linked to defined sales objectives over a three-year period.

With bonuses, employers may have very different ideas to yours, and you should allow for this fact. Listen, therefore, to any counter proposals that are put forward. Staying flexible is important.

Reviewing bonus arrangements

Some management consultants express the view that the life span of any bonus should be no more than 5 years. This could be a case of consultants preparing the ground for repeat business! Nevertheless, there is some truth in the observation that, with bonuses, sooner or later the gloss starts to wear off. The incentive wears off. The reward is taken for granted. The bonus only becomes a matter for conscious thought when it doesn't pay enough.

The message here is that, at some point in the future, you will probably want to revisit your bonus – hence the importance of periodic review. As far as you can, therefore, condition your employer into accepting the view that the bonus isn't for ever. It is relevant to today's circumstances but tomorrow may be a completely different story.

Questions and answers

Bonus ceilings

Q *I have put forward a proposal for part of my salary to be linked to the amount of new business I bring in. Whilst my employers have gone along with the proposal, they want to put a ceiling on the amount of bonus I can earn. I guess the problem is they're scared I could be earning more than my boss. However, since my boss is paid a straight salary irrespective of how much effort he puts in, I don't view this as being particularly fair. Do you agree?*

A Fair or not, you could be left with a take it or leave it situation. Whether your boss's salary is the problem or whether the ceiling is to prevent your bonus from spinning out of control is neither here nor there. Having exhausted negotiation on the imposition of a ceiling, perhaps the next angle you need to pursue is putting a floor in place as a kind of *quid pro quo*, i.e. a minimum level beneath which your bonus earnings cannot sink. The net effect will be to compress the range over which your earnings could vary but, at the same time, it will ensure that you're not being left with more than your fair share of the risk.

My employers are seeking to buy out my bonus

Q *Six months ago I negotiated a performance-related element into my pay and, as a result, I made a lot of money. My employers have now come along and said they want to consolidate the bonus back into my salary. Whilst the figure they've mentioned is not unreasonable, it falls a long way short of what I could earn if the bonus remained. Do I have to accept what they're suggesting or is there some other course of action open to me?*

A This sounds like a bonus that has gone out of control (for whatever reason). Your employer may have little choice other than to try and buy it back from you. Do you have to accept? Contractually speaking, the answer is no. By the same token, digging your heels in may not be a very sensible course of action either (we're sure we don't have to spell this one out to you!). Really, your best route would be to try to come to an agreement with your employer on the terms for buying out your bonus (i.e. get the best deal you can). In addition to the consolidation, perhaps they could also make a one-off payment to you as compensation for any immediate short fall you see. As to your bonus, take the view that it was good while it lasted. It sounds like it was destined to be short-lived anyway.

Problems with peers

Q *I am one of five regional managers and, whilst my company is not averse to the idea of putting me on performance related pay, they don't want me on different pay arrangements to my four colleagues. The bottom line here is that my performance far outstrips the rest so I have the sneaking feeling that what suits me isn't going to suit them. Any suggestions as to how I move this one forward?*

A It sounds like you're flogging a dead horse. Perhaps you would be better off putting your effort into negotiating an improved salary based on your excellence i.e. forget the bonus plan.

Work with no easily measurable output

Q *I happen to be a Human Resources Manager and, picking up on the point you make in the text, my work has no easily measurable output as far as I can see. Does this mean that going onto bonus isn't for me?*

A We have heard of human resources specialists being paid bonuses based on measures of performance such as attainment of recruitment targets and completion of projects but on the whole we share the view that there are some areas of work where performance pay poses more problems than it solves.

Summary

Going onto bonus commends itself particularly to those who are in positions where the results of their work are measurable in some convenient way. Top of the list still are people in sales but, with the move towards greater empowerment and profit accountability right across the board in organizations, the scope for performance-related pay is widening all the time.

Don't be too put off by the risk element. View the ups and downs in earnings as part of the fun of it and, more importantly, adapt your lifestyle to make hay when the sun shines and to tighten your belt when times are hard. The secret here is not to notch up your overheads every time you hit a good spell. Learn instead to ride the peaks and troughs by having Fully Flexible Finances (as far as you possibly can).

In negotiating performance-related elements into your pay, take into account that your employers may not share your enthusiasm for the idea – indeed they may need some persuading. Prepare your case carefully and thoroughly. Be ready to explain what's good about performance-related pay – both for them and for you.

Finally, don't view your performance-related pay as a permanent feature. Some day you may want to go back onto a straight salary – or else change the performance measures to ones more appropriate to your new circumstances. Provide for this eventuality by having your escape route prepared in the form of a periodic review.

Verdict on going onto bonus

Good points

Again, this is a way forward when rigid salary structures stand in the path of pay progression. Given effort and in favourable circumstances (in which you have ultimate control over a lot of the performance factors), the pay offs can be very good indeed.

Bad points

It could be hard to gain approval from your employer, particularly if there are entrenched attitudes towards bonuses. It could also lead to difficulties for you if your finances are not very flexible.

6 | EMPIRE BUILDING

Taking more and more responsibilities under your wing has the effect of increasing your silent bargaining power. For those who are hungry for more pay, it offers yet another alternative. Drawing together some of the lessons in earlier chapters, we want to take a look at:

- Opportunities for empire building – organizational structures and the clues to look for
- How to go about extending your remit – self-empowerment
- Empire building skills – what it takes to be successful
- Bringing the silent bargaining power to bear
- Empire building in small and unstructured organizations

What is empire building?

Empire building is not a term we readily associate with the modern world. Its appearance in a book like this may, therefore, come as a surprise to some readers. However, it is a term that has a place in modern business, as we shall see.

Empire building is the art of bringing more and more under your control. The automatic, knock-on effect this has on our silent bargaining power is what interests us here of course.

Favourable conditions for empire building

Let's start by defining the kind of conditions that are favourable for empire building. These are found in organizations where:

- people are working under pressure
- job boundaries are flexible
- offers to take on more responsibility are welcome.

Situations such as these are ripe for exploitation. The following case study helps to show how.

CASE STUDY: ELLEN

Ellen works for a small company which has tripled its turnover in the last 2 years. Ellen started as a PA. Then, as the business grew, she took over responsibility for all the order processing and general sales administration, recruiting her own team of people. Six months ago, the Systems Manager left half way through a major project and Ellen saved the day by hurriedly stepping into his shoes. Now the Chief Executive is finding she doesn't have time to run the accounts section as she has always done in the past. By volunteering herself, Ellen will soon be adding this to her portfolio too.

What we are seeing here is willing hands at work, making the most of situations in which, because of fast growth, a company is constantly on the verge of splitting at the seams. Given these circumstances, Ellen's offers to take on more work are eagerly grasped. In one instance, her intervention kept the systems department afloat at a time of crisis. In the other, she stepped in when she saw the Chief Executive struggling. Ellen's silent bargaining power has increased enormously from the days when she was a PA. If she ever has occasion to ask for a pay rise, it's a safe bet her case will receive very sympathetic treatment indeed. She would be a very hard person to replace!

Lateral job extension

There is an interesting side issue here. Reading between the lines, Ellen is in a position where she reports directly to the Chief Executive. She is probably one of a handful of senior managers and perhaps someone who is entitled to take the view that her career prospects are restricted. The Chief Executive isn't likely to move on (it sounds like she owns the business) and there is no pyramid of management to climb. What Ellen has done, however, is to promote herself into a bigger job by shifting the boundaries of her existing responsibilities sideways. In effect, she is writing her own job description. She is determining her own place in the structure of the business and she is doing this by making use of the opportunities for **lateral job extension** that have been presented to her. She is empire building very effectively.

Ok, we can hear you saying, but surely there's only so much of this you can do (even if the conditions are favourable). At some point you won't be able to take on any more work. There simply aren't enough hours in the day.

Whilst taking the point that most employees already have enough to do, the general principle to follow here is that, in work terms, what you suck in sideways, you delegate downwards – ensuring of course that it's always you who stays top of the heap. In Ellen's case, she probably recruits more staff to help her discharge her extended functions. Let's face it, Ellen's ability to soak up added responsibilities works greatly in the company's favour so she will probably get the resources she needs (the alternative is recruiting more managers).

Key point

Don't let preconceived ideas about being 'too busy' get in the way of your ambitions. See these lateral job extension opportunities as something to be grasped.

Self-empowerment

Empowerment is a process that normally starts at the top of organizations. Tasks are delegated downwards. People lower down the ladder are given the authority to make decisions – authority they didn't have previously.

Here we are looking at **self-empowerment**, where the process starts from beneath. The driving force is the individual – namely you.

By seizing opportunities to extend your remit through empire building – as Ellen did – you invest yourself with more and more authority. The knock-on effect is big accruals of silent bargaining power.

NOTEPAD

A lot of the points we've covered so far in this chapter share common ground with material we covered in Chapter 4 where we looked at getting promotion. The difference between getting promoted and building empires is that when empire building:

■ you retain your existing responsibilities

■ you're moving across corporate boundaries, rather than up them in straight lines

■ the end job is one you essentially create for yourself.

What it takes to be a good empire builder

Good empire builders are people who:

■ are working for the right kind of organization

■ are good at spotting the opportunities for empire building – notably the gaps that appear when peers leave or start to fall down on the job, or when people higher up the ladder are struggling to cope

■ are quick off the mark (with empire building there is usually a 'window of opportunity' – if you leave it too long, you can find the window has closed and that someone else has beaten you to it)

■ can build a good team of people around them – a team which will be able to help them to deal with the extra work they take on.

Opportunities for empire building in small and unstructured organizations

Changing employment patterns mean that increasing numbers of people work in one of the following:

- **small firms** – these are firms employing less than 50 people.

- **decentralized organizations** – previously large structures have been broken down into a number of small autonomous units, rendering them, effectively, into a series of small firms.

- **delayered and downsized organizations** – people are thinner on the ground than they used to be and more and more work is concentrated into fewer and fewer pairs of hands.

- **high growth organizations** – like Ellen's company, these are organizations where expansion is always threatening to outstrip the capacity of the incumbent management team.

If you go back to the list of favourable conditions for empire building (page 000) you will see that they mirror almost exactly the kind of conditions you find in organizations such as these. In short, they usually have lots of opportunities for lateral job extension. It's back to those magic words again: 'I can do that – leave it to me.'

Bringing the silent bargaining power to bear

This is where we look at reaping the fruits of empire building. How do you convert your newly acquired responsibilities into cash?

First let's look at the wrong way to go about it.

CASE STUDY: SEAN

Sean is the manger of a small sports and leisure complex, part of a group of similar businesses.

A fortnight ago, the manager of another complex in the group was suspended following the discovery of some financial irregularities. Sean was asked to keep an eye on the place pending the results of an investigation by the internal audit team. Pretty soon it became apparent to Sean that with, a bit of reorganizing, he could manage both complexes quite comfortably. Therefore, when it was decided to dismiss the other manager, he approached the Group Chairman to say that he would be happy to run both complexes in return for a 50% hike in his salary. The Group Chairman, however, wrote back declining his offer. Soon after, Sean saw the job advertised in the newspaper.

By laying down conditions (namely an up-front pay increase) Sean invited a negative response. His Chairman undoubtedly read the threat between the lines – that Sean wouldn't take on the added responsibilities unless the money was paid up front first. He reacted accordingly and, in polite terms, told Sean what to do with his idea.

The mistake? Sean should have put his proposal forward without the condition. The key points to pick out here are that:

■ Increased silent bargaining power is part of the harvest of empire building. What Sean attempted to do was to try to use it before he'd even managed to acquire it.

■ Sean may or may not have got a pay rise for taking over the management of both complexes. Whatever the financial outcome, the aim (empire building) would have been achieved .

■ The fruits of empire building in the shape of more leverage come later – in Sean's case when he'd proved he could run both complexes without any hitches.

Questions and answers

Job extension – letting the company take advantage of me

Q *Knowing the principals in my organization, they'd be really pleased if I volunteered to take on more responsibilities without any extra pay. Isn't what you're suggesting playing straight into their hands?*

A The way to look at it is as follows. The fact that your principals are happy to let you build an empire is good news as far as you are concerned. You're adding to your value and enhancing your silent bargaining power. The pay off will come later when you put in for a pay rise and use you proven track record with your new responsibilities to justify your case. In short your principals will have played into your hands – the very opposite to what you are suggesting.

Failed empire building

Q *I recently took over responsibility for the logistics department in addition to my normal duties as Materials Manager. On the whole this hasn't worked out very well. I have now reached the point at which I think it would be sensible to have words with my boss, the Manufacturing Manager. Before I embark on this step, however, is there any advice that might be useful to me?*

A First, make sure that you're not making a hasty judgement. Is there any way you could find out how your management of the logistics department is viewed in the organization? A way of doing this is by tapping into your networks. Is there anyone in the firm who could carry out the soundings for you? Emphasize the purpose of your line of enquiry, so your contact understands you are looking for honest opinions. Given that your view is confirmed (i.e. that your management of the logistics department has not been very successful), an early discussion with your boss is indeed advisable. Here, seek to explore the alternatives (the fact that you have come clean with employers usually means you stand a fair chance of getting them on your side). It could be, for example, that your boss has some ideas on how you could tackle things differently. Don't, under any circumstances, feel that all is lost.

Where you're asked to take on more responsibilities

Q *Isn't there a world of difference between volunteering yourself for extra responsibilities and having them foisted on you? With the former, I can well understand that it would be wrong to ask for the money up front first but with the latter surely an increase in salary should form part of the deal?*

A The important point here is not to let arguments about minor adjustments in your pay get in the way of massive accumulations of silent bargaining power. Even if the extra responsibilities have been dumped on you with little choice, even if your employer's lack of largesse leaves you feeling astounded, don't miss out on the chance to build up the size of the leverage you can bring to bear on the corporate purse – leverage that will pay you back handsomely in years to come. This is a case of learning to play the long game rather than getting bogged down with trivial issues before you even get to first base.

Empire slipping away

Q *Twelve months ago, the board asked me to take on responsibility for a loss-making division in addition to running my own. The previous divisional manager had left under a cloud and the board didn't want to rush into making a new appointment until they had had the chance to assess the situation properly. In short, it seemed like a perfect opportunity for empire building hence I put everything I'd got into the loss-making division and eventually succeeded in turning it round. Imagine my disappointment, therefore, when I found out that the board had decided to recruit a new divisional manger and had briefed a firm of head-hunters to find someone suitable. Where did I go wrong in my attempt to build up silent bargaining power? Please explain.*

A It sounds like your board have simply gone through with their original intentions i.e. to let you do a care-taking job on the loss-making division and to appoint a replacement for the errant manager only as and when the business appeared viable. The mistake? Your board doesn't seem to be aware that you had permanent designs on the job. In short, your aim (empire building) was under-communicated. Don't give up just yet, however. Even at this late stage it may still be possible to salvage the situation. Make your aim known. Remember, thanks to your efforts, you now have substantial silent bargaining power on your side.

Summary

Empire building is only possible where the conditions allow. In a lot of larger, more structured organizations it simply wouldn't be on to start taking over other departments *en masse*, and you would be viewed with suspicion if you attempted to do it. Given, however, that favourable conditions do exist, empire building offers a way of accumulating silent bargaining power in very substantial chunks. Someone like Ellen, for example, is very key to the way her organization works and, if she wasn't there, life for her Chief Executive would be much more painful. Her implied threat of leaving would, therefore, exert considerable leverage on the corporate purse – in short, it's far, far easier to keep someone like Ellen happy and smiling.

Verdict on empire building

Good points

Building an empire is a way of amassing quite substantial amounts of silent bargaining power. It lends itself to many contemporary career situations, e.g. flat organizations, small firms and high growth enterprises.

Bad points

It could lead you to over stretch yourself. Be careful about taking on responsibilities you can't handle.

7 | SHOPPING THE JOB MARKET

If exercising your silent bargaining power hasn't worked, where do you go next? The answer for a lot of people is to try the outside job market – to see what price tag other employers would be prepared to put on their talents. In this chapter we want to look at:

- The risk attached to changing jobs and how you should view it
- Targeting job search – focusing on jobs where the money is going to match up to what you are looking for
- Cutting down on time wasting
- The job market divided into its visible and invisible parts – making sure you're tapping into both
- Putting together a CV that will help you to source well-paid jobs
- Negotiating pay with new employers – how to get the best deal for yourself
- How to deal with pay enticement – when all that glitters is not gold

Managing the risk

The risk of changing jobs

Changing jobs is intrinsically risky and, first and foremost in a lot of people's minds, is the fear that the new job might not work out for them – then where would they go? A case study will help to draw out some of the points you need to consider before deciding to pursue your pay ambitions on the outside job market.

CASE STUDY: CRAIG

Craig works for a company which has gone through the trauma of several changes of ownership over the past 5 years. This, coupled with indifferent trading results, has led to poor pay increases recently. Now Craig, like most of the rest of the staff, is very dissatisfied with his salary. Whereas a number of his colleagues have already left, Craig is not so sure about following in their footsteps. Yes, his pay may be poor, but at least he has the knowledge that his position is relatively secure – something he wouldn't be able to guarantee with a new employer (someone he wouldn't know). Chief among Craig's worries is the fact he is the family bread winner. Apart from the small amount of money his wife earns from a part-time job, his salary has to cover all the household expenses.

In short, Craig sees himself as a person who can't afford to take risks. The likelihood, therefore, is that he will stay where he is. In other words, he will go on being poorly paid.

Is there another option? As with any risk situation, the answer is to view it properly – by which we mean, once again, looking at both the upsides and the downsides.

In changing jobs, the main upside for Craig would be the improvement in his salary. There may be other upsides of course; perhaps his new employer will be able to offer him more in the way of promotion prospects. As to the downsides, these are rooted in the fact that he would be taking a step into the unknown. Irrespective of how much groundwork he puts into researching his new employer, the success or failure of the move rests largely on how well he fits in when it comes to working for them. It could go to plan. On the other hand, it could turn out to be an unmitigated disaster.

When deciding whether the outside job market is for you, there is a further aspect of risk assessment that needs to be carried out – an assessment a lot of people tend to overlook.

The risk of staying in a job

Just as changing jobs is a risk, so is staying put. The upside in this case is the security of knowing who you're dealing with. The downside, though, is continuing to be underpaid and the effect this will have. Not least is the question of the effect on your confidence and self-esteem. Ultimately, of course, it can make you bitter and envious of others.

⚠ WARNING!

Don't see any situation as risk free. Risk is all around us and there's no such thing as playing safe – indeed, attempting to do so is one of the most dangerous things you can do. Staying put in a poorly paid job is particularly dangerous.

Balancing risk and gain

Having accepted the risks that go with changing jobs, what you need to do next is ensure that the downsides and upsides balance. The bottom line here is that you've got to see a tangible gain from a job move. Conversely, you must ensure that you're not changing jobs for trivial increases in your salary. (If the upside isn't good enough, why take the risk?) This contrasts with pay bargaining internally where the downsides are low and where a more modest rise might be acceptable.

NOTEPAD

Be quite clear in your own mind why you're going out onto the job market. If your pay grouses are minor or if their origins are very recent, it may be better to think twice. To repeat a point we made earlier on in the book, because of the general riskiness of moving employers, always view going out onto the job market as an action of last, rather than first, resort.

Targeting your salary

This is important. You must have clear idea in your head of the salary you are looking for *before* you set foot in the market place because, if you don't you will find yourself looking at all the wrong stalls. The result? You'll waste an awful lot of time and the overall experience will be discouraging. Discouragement, incidentally, is the most common reason for giving up. You must never allow yourself to get discouraged.

This leads us to the first area of difficulty you will find you face when you go out on the job market. What kind of figure should you be asking for? With your own employer you stand a fair chance of knowing what's realizable and what isn't, but with the outside market where do you go to for guidance? In most cases you can access three sources:

- **Your networks** – what people you know tell you about available salaries.

- **Your reading** – what you learn about salaries for people with your range of skills and experience from scanning the job ads in the newspaper.

- **Your experience** – the feedback you pick up from applying for jobs, in particular any feedback that suggests you may be looking for too much. Of course, experience is something you can only accumulate as you go along.

Banding your pay aspirations

With information sourced from networking contacts, it is important to distinguish between fact and opinion. For instance, opinion can be distorted by a particular individual's way of seeing things. Perhaps a contact also has a salary problem and, by saying to you that there's stacks of money to be had out there, they may be seeking to reassure themselves that this is the case. Really, they have no better insight into the situation than you have. Even when the information is factual it may not be typical of what's available on the market (perhaps only what one or two employers pay). You have no way of knowing, of course, whether a particular salary is on the high side or the low side of what's available – or whether it's somewhere in the middle. In short, networked information may not help you very much when it comes actually to picking a figure to go for.

Similarly, advertisements in newspapers may not be too helpful. Those that quote salaries and that are seeking people with similar skills and experience to yours may be fairly thin on the ground. Again, you will be left having to guess whether these salaries are on the high side or the low side of the market, or whether they are somewhere in between.

Because of these uncertainties and because of your lack of first-hand job market experience, it is usually a good idea to band your salary aspirations at the start, rather than to try to pick a specific figure. The top of the band should equate to your 'best hope' and the bottom should be the minimum figure for which you would be prepared to move (consistent with the need to make a tangible gain from changing employers). The band you arrive at gives you a basis on which to approach the market and to carry out negotiations with employers. Trying to do this detailed analysis on your feet is tricky to say the least. Trying to do it eyeball-to-eyeball with an employer at an interview is asking for trouble. Be prepared.

Start on the high side

We say this for two reasons:

  1 It's easier to come down than it is to go up.
  2 Who knows, you may come across someone who is happy to pay you your best hope!

This figure is now your **pay target**. It is a figure you may adjust in the light of experience – particularly experience that is telling you that you may be asking for too much.

NOTEPAD

The modern job market is very diverse. Gone are the days when the salaries paid for certain jobs were dictated by a few large firms within given areas or trades. Gone, very often, are the large firms themselves. In their place a patchwork quilt of mainly smaller employers has sprung up – many of whom compete quite ferociously, especially for people with sought-after experience and skills. The result is a supply-led market where salaries are often determined by people going along to companies and naming their price – which employers either agree to or use as a basis for negotiation (downwards). If you are seeking to maximize your salary potential, therefore, it is this kind of market you need to be ready for. In other words, the point at which the bargaining kicks off is often left up to you. This applies to people at any level in any industry where skill, know-how and experience are at a premium.

Putting together a CV to target the right jobs

A CV is essential these days and you won't get very far without one. Most of you will already have a CV and those of you who haven't should take urgent steps to prepare one. A CV is there to give employers a clear idea of who you are and where you're coming from, all in one quick and easy read. A CV needs to communicate enough information to determine whether you fit in with what the employer has got to offer or not. If you do, great. If you don't, then you don't want to waste any more of their time and, equally, you don't want them to waste any more of yours.

> **WARNING!**
>
> Never view a CV as a tool to pull the wool over someone's eyes.
> If you're not suitable for a job, it's as much in your interests as the
> employer's to make sure this is deduced as soon as possible.

If you are on the job market for more pay, it is extremely important
to transmit this information through the medium of your CV. If the
information isn't there, you've got no one to blame except yourself
if you end up in time-wasting interviews for jobs where the pay
falls way below the figure you're targeting.

How do you get this information onto your CV? CVs don't come in
any standard form, of course, but usually there is a section in which
you set out a short résumé of yourself or a place where you describe
the kind of opportunity you are seeking. This is where you need to
insert the exact figure you are looking for (your pay target). Don't
have qualms about doing this. Employers need to decide for
themselves whether they can afford you or not, and it's in your
interests as much as theirs that they get this decision right.

The job market

The **visible job market** is the one we're all familiar with – the jobs
that are advertised in newspapers and journals, or on employers'
web sites. Finding out about them is simply a matter of keeping
your eyes open. There is, however, another job market – one that is
less easy to penetrate – and it is on this **invisible job market** that
you will find some of the best opportunities.

What is the invisible market?

Roughly speaking it's all the jobs that aren't advertised. Into this
category come:

- jobs that are filled by employers making direct
  approaches to people, including (a) people known to
  employers through the trades in which they operate and
  (b) people whose CVs they have on file

- jobs that are created by people approaching employers (positions are created specially for them)
- jobs that are filled by people supplied by consultants of various kinds.

Finding ways of accessing this lucrative but invisible market presents a special challenge to anyone aspiring to maximize their pay potential by changing jobs. Put simply, it's something they can't afford to miss out on. This is a subject we will return to a little later.

Targeting the visible market

Jobs that are advertised fall into two categories:

- jobs where the salary is clearly stated
- jobs where there is no mention of salary or where terms like 'negotiable' or 'commensurate with the responsibilities' are used.

With the first category there is no problem whatsoever. From the figure quoted you will be able to see whether the salary matches up to your target. If you like what you see, you can proceed accordingly.

⚠ WARNING!

If you find the figure quoted in an advert is greater than the figure you've put in your CV, adjust the latter accordingly. This is important for two reasons:

1 Some employers use CV reading software which is programmed to search for key words or information. A misaligned salary expectation, therefore, means that your CV could end up on the reject pile before it's even been scrutinized by human eye.

2 To some employers, a salary expectation lower than the one they're advertising conveys the image of someone who's not really up to the job.

But what about the second category of advertised jobs – the ones where there's no indication of the salary? How do you know whether the job's worth applying for or not?

There are four main reasons why employers don't put salaries in ads:

1 Secrecy – they don't like the idea of everyone knowing the salaries they pay.
2 Their salaries are poor.
3 Their ideas on salary are flexible.
4 They're fishing in the dark – they don't know what kind of price to put on the job and they too are shopping the market.

What you don't know, of course, is exactly which kind of animal you're dealing with. This, however, is where your revised CV comes into play. Any employer reading it will be able to see if their ideas on salary match up with yours, meaning your application goes no further if the figure they've got in mind falls short of the expectation you're flagging up.

NOTEPAD

A difficulty here is that applicants usually end up getting the standard 'sorry but no thank you' letter, conveying the impression that they're not suitable for the job for some unknown reason (few employers actually tell candidates that they can't afford them). 'Sorry but no thank you' letters sow the seeds of discouragement and one of the reasons for proper targeting is to ensure you don't get too many of these – in other words this is an unfortunate spin-off of the process. When replying to ads without salaries, try telling yourself that there's a 75% chance the salary is lower than the figure you're looking for. Similarly, with any 'sorry but no thank you' letters you get back, take it as read that there's a 75% chance the problem is the job not you. Mainly, don't get discouraged.

Targeting the invisible market

Predictably, this is harder than shopping the visible market. It involves:

- ■ targeting employers who are likely to be able to pay you the kind of money you are looking for and approaching them
- ■ targeting the right firms of consultants
- ■ using your networks to access well-paid opportunities.

Let's now look at each of these in turn.

Targeting the right employers

You will probably know a few of these already. After you have been operating in your trade or profession for a number of years, you will know who is likely to have a need for someone with your experience and range of skills. You may also have some insight into what kind of salaries these employers pay. Notorious poor payers can, of course, be struck off your list straightaway. Don't waste any time on them.

You can add to the pool of employers you are targeting in several ways:

- ■ Keep an eye on ads in newspapers. In particular, look out for employers who are advertising for people with similar skills and experience to you (the jobs may not be an exact match, but it tells you there's a reasonably good chance they may have a slot for you somewhere).
- ■ Look out for employers who are recruiting generally (indicating organizations that are in growth).
- ■ Identify employers who advertise jobs with good salaries (these are the top payers who you need to target).
- ■ Tap into your networks. Bearing in mind all we've said previously about the dangers of information sourced via networks, see if any of your contacts know of employers who may have a need for someone like you.
- ■ Research trade directories. These are the kinds of publication that might be on the reference shelves of your local library (or your company might keep copies).

Having got your list of targeted employers together, next you need to make contact with them. You can do this in two ways:

1 **Cold call them** – simply pick up the phone and give them a ring. The person you need to speak to is the person who would have a direct interest in someone with your experience and skills – for instance if you're an accountant the right person to speak to would be the Financial Manager, and so on. Get this person's name from whoever answers the 'phone. Don't be fobbed off with the name of the Personnel or Human Resources Manager. Personnel departments get too many calls from people like you – also they wouldn't be the people to benefit directly from the skills and experience you can offer. When you have made contact with the right person, spell out quickly the reason for your call, i.e. give a brief résumé of who you are and what you're looking for (name the figure).

2 **Send a copy of your CV** – again get the name of the right person (by 'phoning up and asking). Address your correspondence to this person by name and mark your envelope 'Confidential'. This usually ensures that the right person opens it. A short accompanying letter will help – just to explain briefly the reason why you're sending in your CV (i.e. to see if there is anything suitable for you). You can use your accompanying letter to re-state your salary ambitions. This ensures the main point isn't missed.

You mustn't expect cold calling or sending in your CV to yield immediate results but the unexpected does sometime happen – as this next case study illustrates.

CASE STUDY: MARIANNE AND SOPHIE

Marianne works in a very specialist field, designing control systems used on special purpose machine tools. She feels she is underpaid by her present employer and the feedback she gets from her contacts in the trade suggests that much better salaries are available elsewhere. On this basis she decides to put in a call to ABC Developments, a major player in the industry.

Marianne's call is taken by Sophie who is the Control Systems Manager of ABC. Sophie listens very carefully to what Marianne has to tell her about her experience and she realizes straight away that, although she has no vacancies for design staff at the moment, someone with Marianne's background would normally be very hard to recruit. As for salary, Marianne is seeking a figure which is considerably more than she's currently earning and whilst Sophie sees her aspirations as being a little on the high side, she feels that there could be some room for negotiation. What's chiefly at the back of Sophie's mind, though, is that there are plans to expand the design office early next year – by which time Marianne may no longer be available. Taking a note of Marianne's home telephone number and telling her she'll get back to her, Sophie considers her next move. She decides in the end to put up a case to the Chief Executive for recruiting a new member of the design team now, rather than leaving it until January then finding no one suitable applies. She feels confident she will have no problem getting the Chief Executive to agree to this.

The points to pick out from this case study are as follows:

- If Sophie is successful in steering her plan past the CEO and in agreeing terms with Marianne, the vacancy for a control systems designer with ABC Development will never surface in the visible job market.

- This is typical of 'modern market' situations. Busy managers like Sophie are happy to grab lifelines that are presented to them in the form of quick and easy solutions to imminent problems, like trying to recruit someone with scarce or specialist skills.

- Marianne's current earnings influenced Sophie's view of what she might eventually be prepared to accept (a point we will be looking at later on in this chapter).

Marianne had a stroke of luck, of course. Her approach to Sophie came at just the right time, whereas the usual outcome of cold calling and sending in your CV is to sow a few seeds.

When cold calling, the object of the exercise is to learn something from the feedback you get from the voice contact. Is this employer ever likely to have the kind of opportunities you're looking for? Does the pay figure you mention frighten them? Do vacancies come up frequently or are they few and far between? These are the kind of questions you need to be asking. From the answers, you will be able to form an assessment of whether it will be worth ringing this employer again. When you are cold calling a number of employers, it is a good idea to do this assessment by scoring them on a scale of 0 to 5. High scorers will be the employers you will be ringing fairly regularly, whereas those in the 2 to 3 bracket may only warrant a call every 6 months or so. Strike off the really low scorers. They're simply not worth the effort of contacting again, but more importantly, you'll be focusing your sights on a more defined target, i.e. fewer employers. Sooner or later, persistence will pay off for you.

When sending in your CV there is no voice contact of course and hence no feedback. What you're hoping for here is that the CV will get stored in a safe place (one from where it will be retrieved if something suitable should come up). Don't bank on this happening, however. Don't expect to get a reply to your unsolicited letter either. If you do, you'll find the absence of response has a discouraging effect on you (discouragement, remember, can be the cause of giving up prematurely).

What about faxing your CV or e-mailing it? On the whole, we would advise against this for two reasons:

1 Especially with faxes, there is the chance of your CV going astray.

2 For the trick to work, your CV must be in a durable form, i.e. the kind of form that will survive being in a pile on someone's desk for several months!

Targeting the right firm of consultants

A lot of invisible market recruitment goes on through agencies or consultants of various kinds. You must get your name and details onto the databases of the right firms. How do you know which ones to choose?

The number of recruitment businesses operating in any given area can be staggering, to say the least. Not surprisingly, therefore, a lot of people find themselves confused when it comes to selecting the right firms of consultants to register with.

How to proceed? Here is a plan of action for you to follow:

1 Tap into your networks. Have any of your contacts (those with similar skills and experience to you) had recent dealings with firms of consultants? If so, can they pass on any recommendations to you?

2 Scan the ads in the newspaper. Recruitment consultants often advertise vacancies on behalf of their clients and, from these advertisements, you will see which firms of consultants deal with people like you.

3 Look through the listings in business telephone directories. You will see many firms of recruitment consultants actually state what kind of appointments they handle. If in any doubt, a quick phone call will soon settle the matter one way or the other.

 WARNING!

Don't register with too many consultants at the same time or you may find yourself with too many interviews. Six consultants is probably the maximum.

Registering with a firm of recruitment consultants usually involves filling in a registration form and attending an interview. Depending on the consultants (and on the kind of work you do), you may also be required to do an aptitude test. Make sure the recruitment consultants understand what you're seeking to gain from a change of jobs. Where pay is the main issue, you need to make this crystal clear to them. Usually, a space is provided on the registration form for stating your salary requirements. In addition, anything you say in face-to-face interviews must emphasize the fact that pay is the over-riding item on your agenda.

If all goes to plan, the consultants will be able to use their know-how and connections to find you a job paying the right kind of money. You will have opened up another port of entry into the elusive invisible market.

But what happens if the recruitment consultants come up with nothing? What do you do when the phone doesn't ring?

Stony silences tend to mean one of two things:

1 The recruitment consultants are useless.
2 The level of pay you are seeking isn't available on the market.

With the first, you can always register with another firm of consultants. With the second, you may need to revisit your pay target and adjust it in accordance with your experience (reviewing pay targets is a subject we will be looking at shortly). A useful way of putting your finger on the problem is by comparing the performance of all the consultants you are registered with. If someone is performing well and others aren't, this is a tell-tale sign of uselessness. If, however, none of the consultants seem to be coming up with anything suitable, read it as a sign that your sights may be set too high.

NOTEPAD

Recruitment consultants who pester you with vacancies that fall way short of the mark are generally bad news. It's a sign they're desperate to get sales commissions, meaning they're not proceeding with your best interests at heart. Sever your links with them.

Using your networks

This is the last of the three ways of accessing the invisible market – 'phoning round your contacts to see if they know of any suitable opportunities for you and, if necessary, getting your contacts to put out feelers for you.

In an informal survey we carried out a few years ago, we discovered that over 50% of people applying for junior and middle management posts in the engineering industry found what they wanted by tapping into their contacts, which emphasizes what a powerful force networking can be. It also demonstrates the value of having contacts who work for other employers – people who can ease you in through the back doors. Such contacts tend to be established in one of three ways:

- **Through your work** – you will have dealings with people who work for other organizations, e.g. customers, suppliers etc.

- **Through outside activities** – this includes membership of professional associations (you can strike up contacts by attending the local meetings). It also includes people you come into contact with through your leisure time activities or by going on courses.

- **Through former colleagues** – these are people you once worked with and who have now moved on (people you have kept in contact with).

When sourcing jobs by networking, an important point to grasp is the need to keep control over what's going on. In particular you need to:

- brief contacts on exactly what you are expecting them to do for you. If it is to effect introductions then they need to be clear what message you want them to put across on your behalf – including the level of pay you are seeking.

- emphasize confidentiality (your contacts may move in the same circles as you do and you won't want it generally known that you're shopping the market).

■ tell your contacts how far you want them to go for you. In most cases this will be to effect the introductions, then hand over to you. Problems can arise when contacts start trying to negotiate on your behalf. Often they do this because they feel they're helping you.

NOTEPAD

An important aspect of networking is that it involves two-way traffic. In other words, what someone does for you, you must also be prepared to do for them in return. This is a sharp reminder to you that you need to be very careful about who you get onto networking terms with. Unsatisfactory people or people who could let you down are certainly best avoided. Otherwise you may find yourself having to make polite excuses to wriggle out of helping them.

Reviewing your pay target

This is something you may have to do in the light of experience. It emphasizes, again, the importance of being flexible.

If you reach a point where you are having no joy at all shopping the outside market, it could be a signal to you that your pay target is too high, i.e. that what you are looking for is not available on the market or it is only available very occasionally.

You need to consider whether to tweak your pay target down a few notches, or whether to carry on as you are for a little longer. First, however, beware of **false readings**.

False readings

False readings can arise where there are other reasons for your lack of success; reasons that have nothing to do with your pay targeting and don't occur to you until someone points them out to you. Here is a little checklist to go through *before* you rush into adjusting your sights downwards.

- How's the economy performing at the moment? Could it be that jobs are generally thin on the ground and this is the reason why you have had no joy?

- Are you looking for work in a very narrow or specialist field? If so, well paying jobs may not come up that often. In short, what you are experiencing is the normal level of market demand for people with your skills and experience.

- Is your CV up to scratch? Could it be that you are unintentionally putting employers off by presenting yourself poorly? A way to check this out is by getting a second opinion. It will help if you know someone who has worked in the recruitment field. Alternatively, buy a book on CV preparation.

- Is there some other factor that might make an employer view you as an unsuitable candidate? A case we came across recently was a candidate who had moved jobs five times in the last 3 years. It was this that was putting employers off rather than, as he thought, the level of pay he was seeking.

- Are you placing too much reliance on the visible market, i.e. jobs that are advertised? The problem with visible market jobs with good pay is that they attract large numbers of applicants. In other words, competition could be the reason you're not having much luck, rather than your pay aspirations. The answer? See if you can do more to tap into the invisible market where competition is not an issue. Follow the advice in this chapter.

Finally, have a word with a few of the recruitment consultants you are dealing with and ask them for an honest opinion on why they've not been able to find much for you. Recruitment consultants should have a good feel for what's attainable and what isn't as far as pay is concerned.

NOTEPAD

If you do decide to adjust your pay target in the light of experience then don't forget:

■ to alter your CV

■ to advise your new target to any recruitment consultants acting on your behalf.

Negotiating pay with prospective employers

As we have seen, any success you have with internal pay negotiation is likely to be based on the exercise of silent bargaining power. Not so, however, with prospective employers. You won't have this kind of lever on them because you're not yet part of their set up – the implied threat of leaving has no relevance to the situation. Factors which can weigh heavily in external bargaining are where:

■ the skills and experience you are offering are ones the employer desperately needs

■ there is no alternative to you – meaning that, if you turn the job down, they will have to go back to square one with their recruiting.

These factors, if you like, make up a different kind of silent bargaining power. The levers you're operating are not the same ones, but the arm-twisting is there nevertheless.

Assessing your bargaining strength

How do you assess the power you have when dealing with prospective employers? One vital clue is provided by looking at how you sourced the job.

Bargaining for visible market jobs

If you have applied for a job you have seen advertised and if the job is a good job, it is a pretty safe assumption that you won't be the only face in the frame. The likelihood is the reverse in fact – that there will be considerable and quite formidable competition for the job. In short, read into this that your bargaining power is likely to be weak.

Bargaining for invisible market jobs

With some invisible market jobs that you source, there will be no competition. This applies particularly to jobs you source by networking or by cold calling employers. You could easily be the single runner in a one horse race – in other words, providing you don't stumble, you can't fail to win. Since there is no alternative to you, your bargaining power is therefore very strong.

With invisible market jobs sourced for you by recruitment consultants, however, absence of competition can't be taken for granted. For instance:

- the recruitment consultants may have put up other candidates apart from you
- the employer may be using more than one firm of recruitment consultants
- in addition to using recruitment consultants, the employer may also be advertising the position.

How do you find out? One way is by asking the recruitment consultants to tell you if other applicants are being seen (there is no reason for withholding this information from you).

With a job you have sourced by mailshotting a copy of your CV, the situation is a little harder to determine. Indeed, the interview may be the first opportunity you get to find out whether there are any other candidates in the field. Sometimes the employer volunteers this information as part of a general briefing on the selection procedure for the job. Sometimes you may have to ask.

Key point

Knowing whether you're up against competition is important to you because it has a bearing on how advisable it is for you to stick out for what you want.

Handling discussions

Because you've transmitted your pay ambitions clearly (through the vehicle of your CV and by other means) any employers who get into discussions with you will be fully aware of what you are seeking to achieve. In theory, this should mean that you will only be getting into discussions with employers who are happy to go along with your aspirations. Your targeting has worked and you've cut out time wasters in the shape of employers who can't or won't deliver.

But this isn't to say that some employers will try to negotiate a lower figure with you, especially if they feel your ambitions are slightly over the top. Negotiate, remember, is what Sophie had in her mind to do with Marianne.

Sticking out for what you want

Negotiation has a simple point to it. You are seeking to find out the employer's best offer, to see whether it fits in with your banded pay target. If it does – and if all other things are equal – then you shake hands on the deal. If it doesn't, then there's no point in pursuing the matter any further.

The battle here is again one of credibility. Do employers believe you're serious about the figure you're asking for or do they think you're trying it on? The opinion they form as a result of talking to you determines how they move forward with the negotiation. At the start, therefore, you need to convince them that you are indeed serious.

NOTEPAD

People who are genuinely underpaid face the greatest challenge of all when it comes to convincing employers that they are serious with what looks like a relatively high bid. Employers will tend to feel that they can be bought for a much lower figure – meaning the offer they make could be a lot less than the offer they'd make to someone earning a higher salary.

How do you deal with this situation? The best way is by letting employers see you know you're underpaid. Be up front about it. Tell them also that just because you're underpaid now doesn't mean you want to go on being underpaid.

The temptation felt by many in the underpaid sector is to inflate their current earnings figure in discussions with employers – just to give a better start point to negotiations. This is a mistake because employers have ways and means of finding out people's earnings in previous jobs. A new employee who has told a few untruths about previous earnings automatically becomes a focus point for suspicion. Needless to say, this won't do you any good at all at a time when you'll be trying to do your best to prove yourself.

Moving the negotiation forward

Let's now view the negotiation from the employer's point of view.

CASE STUDY: PHIL AND JONAS

Phil is the senior partner and major shareholder in a small, specialist IT consultancy which he and two colleagues founded 18 months ago. The business has grown phenomenally since its start up and Phil and his partners are struggling to keep up with the work load.

Jonas's unsolicited CV lands on Phil's desk on a particularly frantic morning, with telephones ringing and e-mails coming in by the dozen. It is not until lunch time, therefore, that Phil gets the chance to read it. Once he has, he sees immediately that Jonas has got some very pertinent skills and experience as far as the business is concerned. The salary he's asking for may be a little on the high side, but there would be many benefits to having an extra pair of hands on board, particularly someone who could deal with clients and troubleshoot software problems.

Phil decides to get Jonas in for a chat. The two of them find they get on well together and, from his point of view, Phil is satisfied that Jonas would fit in nicely.

As to salary, Phil asks Jonas if he is serious about the figure he is asking for. Jonas says he is, pointing to the fact that, apart from the money, he is perfectly happy to stay with his present employer, i.e. he would have no reason otherwise for wanting to move.

After Jonas has left, Phil speaks to his partners. They agree that someone with Jonas's skills would be a great asset to the business and that people like him don't grow on trees. The salary would be a problem, though, not least because Jonas would have to work alongside other employees who are all earning a lot less than the figure he has indicated.

What Phil and his partners have got to decide now is whether to pay Jonas what he wants or to make the best offer they can, consistent with the salaries they are paying to other staff. The following factors are weighing heavily on their minds:

- the scarcity of Jonas's skills (and the difficulty they would have if they ever had to recruit someone like him)
- the fact there is no alternative to Jonas (if he turns their offer down they will be back to where they were before, i.e. snowed under)
- the fact he is 'there'.

By sticking out, Jonas is ensuring that the offer he gets from Phil and his partners will represent the best they can do. It will then be up to him to decide whether it is good enough or not.

NOTEPAD

Sometimes employers like Phil who are constrained in what they can offer you will suggest other ways of making the job attractive. For example:

- a perk, like the kind of car you've only ever dreamed about
- some performance-related element
- an undertaking to pay the money you're asking for at some fixed point in the future, i.e. a two-stage deal
- a golden hello, i.e. a one-off cash lump sum payable to you when you start or in instalments.

The point here is not to dismiss suggestions such as these out of hand. Listen to what's being proposed and think it over carefully. As always, stay flexible. When you reach the point of impasse with an employer, the suggestion to explore some of the other ways mentioned above might have to come from you. Sometimes it doesn't occur to employers that there's more than one way to crack a nut.

Pay enticement

With pay bargaining on the outside job market you need to watch out for employers who are desperate to acquire your experience or skills and who, as a consequence, make you an offer you can't refuse only to find out later that they've overstretched themselves. Overstretching manifests itself in a number of different ways. For example:

- seeking to renegotiate the package.
- no ongoing salary increases (or increases beneath the norm), meaning over a period of time that your salary reverts back to where it was previously
- worst of all, an early termination of the appointment.

The trick is to spot employers who are desperate and to avoid them at all costs. Usually the give away is in the easiness with which the job is offered to you (e.g. at the end of an interview where only a few perfunctory questions have been asked). Another clue is where the employer seems quite keen to 'sell' you the job (e.g. all sorts of rash promises about future prospects are made).

Key point
With jobs, that which glitters frequently isn't gold. See all offers as refusable.

Questions and answers

Well paid but in a dead end

Q *I work for a small firm (five employees) where my prospects for advancement are, practically speaking, nil. Sensing I needed to do something about this, I tried shopping the job market but only to find that every position I applied for paid less than the figure I earn currently. If this is indicating I am highly paid in market terms, where do I go from here?*

A First make sure you're not basing your judgements on too narrow a sample (i.e. just the jobs you've applied for). If we're only talking about a handful, then seek further evidence such as anything you can glean from your networks or by asking a recruitment consultant to give you a view. Other than this, it is not uncommon to find key employees in small companies paid high salaries, simply reflecting the enormous silent bargaining power they have. What to do? Take stock. It could be that you need to take a step sideways or even slightly backwards before you can take one forwards. What you are looking at is your pay prospects in the longer term (prospects that will only open up if you have opportunities for promotion). In other words you may need to look at the bigger picture.

Bidding for more money opens up the risks

Q *Surely the more money I ask for, the more pressure there will be on me to perform. Could I be inviting problems for myself?*

A Alternatively, could you be inviting problems for yourself by continuing to be underpaid? This all comes back to risk and the fundamental point that seeking to play safe is often the most dangerous thing you can do.

Uncomfortable with cold calling

Q *I would feel distinctly uncomfortable about cold calling employers. Isn't there the risk of being seen as a nuisance?*

A If you're cold calling employers every fortnight or so then the answer is clearly yes. As to cold calling generally, look at it this way: recruitment (advertising, using consultants etc.) is an expensive option for employers hence, if you happen to be just what they're looking for, you'll be saving them a lot of money. More importantly, cold calling accesses the invisible market where the best opportunities for making major advances in pay are to be found.

Employers who refuse to put promises into writing

Q *I have been offered a job with marginally more salary than I am currently earning but with the promise of a big increase in six months' time. When I asked the employer to put the promise into writing, however, they refused saying that I would have to take them at their word. How do you view this?*

A Whilst it might be respectable to want to see how someone performs in a job before putting them on a high salary, not being prepared to put the deal into writing invites suspicion about the employer's motives i.e. the promised rise may never materialize. Our advice? There are a few dodgy characters out there on the job market. With this in mind perhaps it would be best to give this particular offer a miss.

Dealing with recruitment consultants

Q *I registered with a firm of recruitment consultants the other day and, to my dismay, the person who interviewed me told me my pay aspirations were totally unrealistic. How do you suggest I should view this information?*

A Normally you would expect recruitment consultants to be in touch with going rates of pay for particular occupational groups within given areas What you must allow for, however, is an individual consultant who is not so well tuned in (lack of experience) or who is trying to condition your aspirations downwards (to make you easier to place). How to proceed? Compare this opinion with the views of other consultants. If the consensus appears to indicate you're going over the top then take action. If not, register yourself with another firm of consultants.

Summary

Changing jobs is not something to be done lightly for these reasons:

- ■ Irrespective of how well you do your research, joining a new employer is still, largely, a step into the unknown. It could go well for you (it usually does) but there is always the risk you won't fit in (it is very hard to predict where this is likely to happen).

- ■ When times are hard, last in is often the first to go. Therefore, when starting a new job you are placing yourself in the position of being at most risk of redundancy.

- ■ You will leave behind all the good work you have done to build up your reputation. You have to start with a new round of impressions. Your Lifelong Interview begins all over again.

- ■ You may lose perks like long service holidays or share options.

- ■ Too many voluntary job moves on your CV can start to look bad. It gives off an image of someone who 'can't settle' or who 'doesn't fit in'.

Because of these factors you should only be contemplating a change of jobs when:

- all internal routes to getting a pay rise have been exhausted
- tangible gains can be made, i.e. don't leave jobs for trivial sums of money
- preferably, some other career objective can also be realized, e.g. a move to a job further up the ladder.

You need to be serious about leaving too. This means you need to have gone through all the downsides in your head like saying goodbye to familiar faces and routines, because it will do you no good at all to find you get cold feet when it comes to handing your notice in. Worse still, is having to withdraw your notice at the eleventh hour. All your credibility will have gone in one fell swoop. It will take you a long, long time to get it back again and, as for silent bargaining power, you might as well forget it.

Having decided to take the plunge into the outside market, you need to be very careful about targeting jobs where the pay is going to come up to expectations. The job market provides endless opportunities for time wasting and chalking up rejections – both of which will only serve to discourage you.

We have given particular attention to the 'invisible' job market where there is often more scope for negotiating good salaries. It is important for you to access this market by following the guidelines in this chapter.

With some experience under your belt, you can tweak your pay ambitions to what the market is capable of providing. You shouldn't be too surprised, however, to find that what's on offer on the market is little if any improvement on what you're already earning. The signal to you is that your pay is perhaps not so out of line as you originally thought. Be prepared for this, that's all. One of the outcomes could be taking the decision that your lot's not such a bad one after all and staying put.

Verdict on shopping the job market

Good points

This is often the quickest way of addressing a pay problem and, done properly, can yield very tangible gains.

Bad points

It is intrinsically risky. With a new employer, it also means you have to build up your silent bargaining power all over again.

8 BLACKMAIL

When seeking to realize pay ambitions internally, we have recommended that you exercise your silent bargaining power. The threats are implied; the words 'I'm off if you don't give me what I want' are understood but never spoken; the levers are very subtle ones. But what if the threats you're making *are* explicit? What if you do actually use the threat to take yourself off to force your employer's hand? What happens then?

In this chapter we're going to look at:

- Blackmail – where it works, where it doesn't and where it can get you into trouble
- Being bought off and where it leaves you
- Unplanned blackmail – where the intention to leave was genuine and where the offer of more money to stay was something you did not expect

Blackmail version one

CASE STUDY: DANIEL AND BRENT

For the last 2 years Daniel has outperformed everyone else in the sales team and this year looks like being the third. The problem for Daniel, however, is that his exceptional performance has not been rewarded to the extent he feels appropriate. He has had salary increases, yes, but in his opinion these are not enough.

After landing yet another major contract, Daniel goes to see his boss, Brent. The gist of the conversation is that Daniel tells Brent he will look for another job if something isn't done about his salary within a fortnight. Daniel is pleased to see that Brent looks shocked.

What we are seeing here is someone whose silent bargaining power should be substantial (a top sales performer) but for whom the technique hasn't worked (or hasn't worked to his full satisfaction).

What will happen now? A lot depends on how seriously Brent takes Daniel's threat. If, for example Daniel is the kind of person who is always threatening to pack his bags and leave, then Brent may not take his threat very seriously at all. As a consequence, he may just sit on his hands. Point one, therefore, is that threats to leave won't do you any good at all unless your employers believe you and this takes us back to the importance of *credibility*. Given, however, that Brent does take Daniel seriously and given too that Daniel's bargaining power is as strong as we think it is, the likelihood is that Brent will be racking his brains trying to think of ways of keeping Daniel happy. And, all things being equal, the likelihood is too that Daniel will get what he wants.

This is Blackmail version one: Daniel didn't actually go out and shop the market. He merely threatened to.

Blackmail version two

CASE STUDY: MEL AND CHRISTIAN

Mel is a top designer and she has been behind a lot of the innovative design ideas that have given her company the competitive edge it currently has in the market place. Mel, however, feels her talents are not sufficiently rewarded – the reason, she guesses, is that if she earns any more money it will put her on a higher salary than some of the senior management team. As confirmation of this fact, another meeting with her boss, Christian, ends with yet more evasive answers of the kind she has heard many times before. So she decides to try a different tack. Next day she rings the Chief Designer of her company's biggest competitor and explains her situation. At the end of the conversation, he invites her to come in for a chat after work and, within 48 hours, Mel has got a very impressive job offer in her hands. She shows this to Christian immediately, signalling at the same time that she intends to accept the offer unless it is matched.

Blackmail version two is done *after* shopping the market. The fact Mel has a job offer in her hands demonstrates to Christian that:

■ she is serious

■ there are employers out there who will pay her what she wants.

Christian now has a stark choice:

1 he gives in to Mel's demands

2 he let's her go to the competition and suffers the consequences.

Where blackmail works

We all know people like Daniel and Mel – people who have got what they want by threatening to leave – so what's to stop everyone using the same technique?

The first point about Daniel and Mel is that both of them have very substantial bargaining power. In Daniel's case, if he left his company, they would lose their top sales performer, while in Mel's case, her design flair would fall into the hands of the competition. There is considerable pressure on both their employers, therefore, to give in to what they want. They may not like the idea of being blackmailed but the downsides of saying no may be too much for them to swallow.

This would not be the case, however, with someone who had rather less in the way of bargaining power. The pressure would not be there to the same degree, meaning the employer would probably balk at being blackmailed, would simply dig in and refuse to shift. Clearly the blackmailer is then in an awkward position. With version one, if they don't carry out the threat to shop the market, their credibility is completely blown. Bargaining power goes out of the window and it will take a long time to get it back again, meaning the employee is in a much worse position than before. A similar situation arises with version two. If the job offer is not taken up, then the individual concerned again loses all credibility.

Key point

Don't make threats to leave unless you intend to carry them out. This means think it through properly first. If you suspect you could get cold feet at the last minute then blackmail probably isn't for you.

⚠ **WARNING!**

With version two of blackmail, bear in mind that an employer who offers you a job will be expecting a fairly prompt reply. If one doesn't arrive, there is the risk that the employer will either (a) cancel the offer or (b) offer the job to someone else (you may not know there is another face in the frame). This could be deeply embarrassing for you if, say, you've been waiting for your firm to come up with a counter offer and one doesn't appear. Blackmailers should note therefore:

■ Any employer who offers you a job needs communication in the form of a quick 'phone call. Since you can't tell them you're using their job offer to blackmail your present employer, an excuse like 'thinking it over for 48 hours' is probably the best one to use. Remember to thank them for their offer at the same time.

■ Similarly, keep your own employers to the same deadlines. Tell them you need an answer quickly (state when).

Snags and blackmail

There are a few problems with using blackmail, as the following list shows:

■ **It leaves a bad taste** – no employer likes being blackmailed and there is an inevitable knock-on effect on your Lifelong Interview. Your image isn't so squeaky clean any more and in some cases it will do damage to your chances of promotion.

■ **It doesn't stand repeated use** – if you threaten to leave every time you want a pay rise, sooner or later it starts to wear thin. Eventually your employers will reach the point where they say to themselves 'enough is enough'.

■ **It can overstretch your employer** – in Mel's case the probable reason for not giving her the pay rise she wanted was the erosion of the (narrow) differential between her salary and the salaries of some of the senior management team in her firm. Given that this is the case and that Mel succeeded in getting what she wanted, it would only be natural for her employers to want to restore the differential as quickly as they can. Mel needs to watch out, therefore, the next time a pay review comes round. She could find herself getting less than the standard rations.

■ **It can give you a bad name on the job market** – employers are quite quick to pick up on individuals who have used their job offers to barter better salaries for themselves. Other than individuals actually volunteering the information, the fact that a perfectly good job offer has been declined tells a tale in itself. The likely reaction? Employers don't tend to fall for the same trick twice. They will be far less accommodating the next time you approach them – indeed it wouldn't be too surprising to find they refuse to have anything to do with you at all.

Unplanned blackmail

CASE STUDY: TESSA AND STEVE

Tessa has been shopping the job market for better pay for some time. Finally, she gets an offer from a good company with a salary she finds very acceptable. Immediately, therefore, she writes out her notice and hands it into her boss, Steve.

Steve's reaction is one of total shock. He asks Tessa if she wants time to think things over to which she replies no – reminding him that he is fully aware she isn't happy with her salary (they've discussed the subject many times). Steve's next question, however, takes her by surprise. He asks her how she would feel if he could match the offer she's received. Thinking quickly, Tessa says she'd consider it certainly and, with that, Steve says he'll get back to her later in the day.

True to his word, Steve speaks to Tessa again just after lunchtime. He says that he's been to see the Chief Executive and the good news is he's been given the authority to match the offer. He tells her to think about it overnight and to let him know her decision next morning.

What a pity it took Tessa's resignation to force a decent salary out of her employers and doubtless this thought will pass through Tessa's head many times as she reflects on Steve's offer overnight. The dilemma she faces is now, however, a difficult one. Either she puts her misgivings about her employer to one side and stays where she is, or she sticks to her original decision to leave (taking on board all the risks that go with changing jobs). Put in this position, most people choose to stay put. In short, they stick with the devil they know.

Any thoughts? Only to say that the realities in cases like Tessa's are that she will probably meet the same resistance again next time she tries to negotiate a pay rise for herself. Indeed. because her pay is now much higher, she could find the resistance even more entrenched.

Questions and answers

Should I reveal my hand?

Q I work in a very tight-knit industry where everyone knows everyone else. This means if I got a job offer from a competitor and showed it to my boss, he would probably ring up the company concerned and accuse them of poaching staff. As this would be embarrassing both for them and for me, wouldn't it be better in this instance to keep the identity of the employer offering me the job to myself?

A Yes it would, without a doubt. The real danger is not so much the embarrassment but the fact that pressure from your boss via the old pals' network could lead to the offer being withdrawn (yes, we've seen it happen in tight-knit industries such as yours). Short of this, it could also give your game away to the other employer, i.e. that you are using their offer for blackmail purposes.

Employers who call your bluff

Q *I put my notice in recently to force my employers to do something about my pay. So far this has drawn no reaction whatsoever and I am getting concerned because I am due to leave in two weeks' time. Could it be that they're calling my bluff? In which case would it be best to stick to my guns right up to the last minute?*

A From what you're saying it's apparent that you don't really want to leave but you've now got yourself into the kind of situation Liam got himself into in Chapter 1. In other words, you've broken the golden rule about making sure you're serious about leaving before putting your notice in. What's the best way out of this? For a start, put an end to this stand-off by broaching the issue with your employer (the sooner you do this, the better). Admit your mistake and ask to withdraw your notice – the alternative is making a job move that you don't really want to make. Ok, so your credibility will have had some of the edges knocked off it but in time and with application you should be able to get this back. On the plus side, coming clean and being honest will hopefully earn you a few brownie points.

Where blackmail is seen to work

Q *Three of my colleagues have recently got substantial rises for themselves by threatening to leave and join competitors. Is there any reason why I shouldn't try to do the same?*

A Yes: for a start they may have more in the way of bargaining power than you and, who knows, your employer may have decided 'enough is enough'. Still pay heed to the advice in this chapter before embarking on this route.

Summary

Blackmail is a high risk game and you shouldn't play it unless:

■ you're 100% confident of your bargaining power

■ you're happy to carry out your threat to leave (i.e. you've thought it through properly).

Given you can put ticks against both of these bullet points, you still need to view blackmail as a blunt-edged weapon which will probably do the job for you but not very cleanly. Notably, you may have to live with some fall out afterwards in the shape of strained relationships with those you report to and attempts to short change you when normal pay review time comes round (employers seeking to restore the equilibrium). Most people who resort to blackmail find they eventually have to leave to realize their full pay potential – reflecting perhaps that they're dealing with employers who only respond when their arms are heavily twisted (employers who are probably limited in what they can provide anyway).

Verdict on blackmail

Good points

Blackmail works where (a) your bargaining power is strong and (b) your credibility is high.

Bad points

It can get you into awkward situations and will probably only work for you once – even then it can leave dents in your image.

9 | GETTING HEADHUNTED

An approach from a head-hunter (or executive search consultant as they're more properly known) is a pretty sure sign that you are about to move into the big league as far as your pay prospects are concerned. Someone, somewhere has identified you as the right person for a top job, meaning the door is wide open for you to negotiate a very good deal for yourself. In this chapter we will be looking at:

- What it takes to get onto head-hunters' lists
- Projecting the right image
- Being visible and marketing yourself effectively
- Dealing with head-hunters – moving approaches forward
- Getting the best deal for yourself – not missing out on the golden opportunity that getting headhunted presents

How headhunting works

On the face of it, being headhunted is an event over which you have no control. The phone call comes out of the blue, the mystery voice at the other end of the line is probably someone you've never spoken to before and the chances are you will probably never find out how he or she got your name.

Executive search has come into its own in the last 25 years to the point where, today, search accounts for a substantial slice of the top jobs market. It is again evidence of the increasing importance of the invisible or unadvertised sector of the market.

Head-hunters start with a clean sheet. A client comes along with a need to recruit executive talent (say, a new CEO), a spec is agreed and the head-hunters take it from there.

Though head-hunters are very secretive about their methods, they are people who spend a lot of time cultivating connections in the business world and it is through these connections that they get the names of suitable candidates. An approach is then made (usually by telephone) and the selection process begins.

If you are being headhunted you will be interested to know that:

■ the jobs are always well-paid jobs (head-hunters' fees alone wouldn't justify their involvement in appointments lower down the ladder)

■ in any event, the salary is usually negotiable

■ you won't be up against too much competition (head-hunters are very selective about who they speak to).

In short, there's a lot in it for you and, if pay's the name of your game, then approach is something you definitely need to be encouraging.

Projecting the right image

Presenting the right image is first and foremost what you must do to get yourself onto head-hunters' lists. The image you project has to be person-perfect and work-perfect and this brings us back to the familiar territory of the Lifelong Interview – the subject we looked at in Chapter 1. Head-hunters get business by reputation and, since the business we're talking about is very lucrative business, they are very keen to distance themselves from anyone who might come across as flawed or sub-standard. This is definitely a case of 'play safe' and it is something head-hunters always seek to do.

Visibility

It goes without saying that being the most person-perfect and work-perfect person in the world won't have much impact if no one knows about you. This brings us next to the very important link between getting onto head-hunters' lists and networking, i.e. your relationship with professional colleagues – people you work with now and people you've worked with in the past; other people you come into contact with in the course of your work; people you meet through going on courses, membership of professional institutions and so on. This is how your person-perfect/work-perfect image gets disseminated to a wider audience and, ultimately, to people like head-hunters, who are very adept at tapping into the networks of others.

NOTEPAD

There is a reminder here that we tend to operate in quite small worlds dictated by our professions and trades (and the areas in which we live). We know A and we know B, and A and B probably know each other, and so it goes on. Anyone who has done head-hunting will tell you just how quickly a list of names can be put together from a few phone calls.

Acquiring experience and skills

This follows on from the lessons in Chapter 2. By adding to your range of experience and skills you add value to yourself, and this value is bankable in the form of enhanced silent bargaining power. Acquiring additional experience and skills also has the effect of making you a more attractive target to head-hunters. Head-hunters are often asked to find people who can bring specialist know-how to businesses and anything you can offer in this area helps to generate approaches.

Marketing yourself effectively

Head-hunters sometimes pick up names from information that is in the public domain. Here is an example.

CASE STUDY: MAXINE

Maxine's company recently received extensive press coverage in connection with a range of eye-catching new products. Maxine, as Marketing Manager, featured prominently in a number of these articles, mainly because she was the person most often in attendance on the company's stand at a major international trade exhibition. Over the next few weeks Maxine received no less than three approaches from head-hunters and she found this remarkable because she had never received an approach from a head-hunter in her life before.

Being linked with 'something good happening' often produces quite remarkable results on the getting yourself head-hunted front – particularly if the something good is newsworthy, i.e. it gets media coverage. In Maxine's case, the new range of products was essentially a combination of innovative design and technical excellence, yet her colleagues in the design and technical departments didn't receive the same attention from head-hunters that she did. This is a case of getting your face in the frame wherever possible.

Receiving approaches

Being headhunted provides you with a golden opportunity to make major strides forward with your salary and you should not miss out on the chance to take advantage of this. The way you receive approaches is therefore important. On the one hand you need to be courteous and obliging; on the other, you have to be careful not to send out any signals that might suggest you're desperate to take the job. In particular:

■ Refrain from making any criticisms of your present employer. Let it come across that, whilst you're always open to offers, you're equally quite happy to stay where you are.

■ On the contrary, enthuse where possible about anything you are doing currently (this is probably what the head-hunter wants to hear anyway).

■ Talk up the price by pointing to what you'll be losing by changing jobs, e.g. continuity of service, pension rights, share options etc. Emphasize that you don't see any of these things as obstacles, providing the opportunity is right – and the package that goes with it, of course.

Moving the approach on

What you are really seeking to do in this first conversation with the head-hunter is to move the approach on to the next stage, i.e. where you get to find out more about the job. What you must not do, therefore, is close any doors. Yes, the approach may have come at a time when you are not thinking about changing jobs, but it is still important that you hear it out. Besides, closing doors could convey the impression to the head-hunter that you're not interested period – meaning they strike you off the call list. The general idea is to keep the approaches coming. If this one's not right for you, then the next one may be.

⚠ WARNING!

When you receive an approach, there is a temptation to tell everyone about it. Don't, for the simple reason that the approach could fizzle out in the early stages – for example, if the head-hunter's client has a change of heart about recruitment and decides to put the exercise on ice instead. The time to start crowing about being headhunted is when you've landed the job. Until this happens, keep it to yourself.

Getting the negotiation going

Moving the approach forward inevitably means going for interviews and being put through various psychological tests. The head-hunters may also ask you to make a short presentation in front of a video camera – the resultant film is something they will show to their clients.

At this early stage in the approach you will find it useful to make a quick assessment of your bargaining strength. This will help you to form a view of the line you should be taking in your negotiations.

With an approach you need to consider your bargaining strength under two headings:

- **Why have you received the approach?** What makes you so special? What you're fishing for here is whether you've got some unique skill or whether there is something in your background and experience which the head-hunter's client puts a particularly high value on. How do you find out? Ask the head-hunter to tell you why you've been singled out? See what you learn.

- **Is anyone else in the running?** The fewer alternatives there are to you, the greater your bargaining strength, and this is something that it is useful to know. Again, ask the head-hunter to tell you what competition you're up against.

Where you see your bargaining strength as high, this is the signal to you to start putting up the asking price.

Naming your figure

'Being greedy' or 'going over the top' has little meaning to people like head-hunters who themselves earn large fees and who are used to talking big salaries without even blinking an eyelid. At the same time, however, expect head-hunters to be quite helpful to you in arriving at a realistic figure. They after all, are going to play a large part in brokering the deal between you and their client.

Here are six golden rules for setting out your pay aspirations to head-hunters:

1 **Be straight** – tell the head-hunter you're seeking to negotiate the best deal for yourself. The head-hunter will view this as perfectly acceptable.

2 **Be ambitious** – don't fall into the trap of asking for too little then finding you could have asked for more later on (when it's too late).

3 **Be clear** – state an actual figure. Don't wrap your ambitions up in vague statements like 'It would take a good offer to tempt me to move'. With something as important as salary, it pays to leave no room for misunderstandings. Where misunderstandings do creep in, it's often hard to get the negotiation back on track.

4 **Be confident** – don't be afraid to name a high price. See yourself as 'worth it'.

5 **Be receptive** – listen to head-hunters. They will tell you if they think you're asking for more than their client will be prepared to pay.

6 **Be consensual** – agree a figure with the head-hunter. Let this be the basis on which the head-hunter presents you to his or her client – the basis on which the negotiation proceeds.

⚠ **WARNING!**

In approach situations, asking for too little can flag up lack of ambition. Needless to say, this will be seen as a bad point if the job you're going after is a top job.

Using head-hunters as a conduit

You can use head-hunters as a go-between when it comes to negotiating the right deal between the employer and yourself. With this, remember:

■ The head-hunter is on client terms with the employer meaning they will usually have a pretty good idea how far the firm can be stretched.

■ The head-hunter has a direct interest in securing a successful outcome to the approach. This is not just in terms of ensuring good client relationships but also because part of their fee is only payable when someone starts in the job.

> **Key point**
> Keep head-hunters on your side. By being helpful and easy to
> deal with you can acquire a very useful ally when it comes to
> getting the best deal for yourself.

Keeping the approaches coming

This is an important part of being head-hunted: make sure it's not a
one-off event. If the job's not right for you, the next one might be,
but the head-hunter has got to want to come back. How do you
keep the approaches coming? Here are some tips:

■ Don't mess head-hunters about. Don't, for example,
   name one salary figure then change your mind later on
   – this will put the head-hunter into a difficult position
   with his or her client. More to the point, perhaps, they
   will start to view you as someone who is indecisive and
   gets cold feet quickly, i.e. not the kind of person a head-
   hunter is keen to deal with.

■ On the contrary, be as helpful as you can at all times. In
   particular, see where head-hunters are coming from.
   See their need to be able to present their client with
   clear and consistent messages.

■ Remember to be courteous. Say thank you.

■ Get back to them when you say you will. Don't leave
   them to chase you.

■ Listen to any advice they give you and, consistent with
   your own aims, try to act on it.

■ If the job's not suitable for you, go to great lengths to
   explain why. If it's the pay, for example, be quite
   specific about what kind of offer it would take to tempt
   you out of the tree. Not only will this brief the head-
   hunter for next time, it will also demonstrate that
   you're not just putting the shutters up (a signal to a
   head-hunter that approaching you is a waste of time).

NOTEPAD

Getting onto head-hunters' call lists means they could also be ringing you for leads from time to time, i.e. to see if you know anyone who they could approach for a job that's landed on their desk. With enquiries of this kind, be as helpful as you can. Even offer to do some of the initial soundings out for the head-hunter (if this is what the head-hunter wants).

Questions and answers

Never been headhunted

Q *I've never been headhunted – why is this?*

A There are many reasons why people don't get headhunted. The following checklist highlights some of the more common ones.

- Are you operating at the top (senior executive) end of the job market? If not, you need to be aware that this is where most headhunting goes on (the cost alone wouldn't justify it otherwise).
- How's the economy performing at the moment? The point here is that the amount of headhunting that goes on declines significantly in recessionary periods when there is a plentiful supply of executive talent on the market and there are easier (cheaper) ways of sourcing it. The message? Don't expect to be headhunted in a slump.
- How do you measure up when it comes to the person-perfect/work-perfect image? Have you blotted your copy book a few times in the past? If so, bear in mind that, with future work at stake, head-hunters aren't inclined to take chances with people.

> ■ Are you known to enough people outside your own organization? If not, your professional network needs expanding. Follow the advice in this book about joining professional institutions, getting involved in activities where people from other organizations will be present etc. Remember you won't get headhunted if no one knows you're there.

Can head-hunters become a nuisance?

Q *Isn't encouraging head-hunters asking for trouble? I don't want consultants ringing me up all the time asking me if I'm interested in such and such a job. I would find it most intrusive.*

A Shutting the door on head-hunters is turning your back on some of the best opportunities the job market has to offer. What's more, with the instability of modern careers, you can never be sure when you're going to need the services of a head-hunter.

Sending head-hunters copies of your CV

Q *With the aim of enhancing my chances of being headhunted is it a good idea to send selected head-hunters a copy of my CV?*

A Not without doing some groundwork first, for the simple reason that head-hunters receive thousands of unsolicited CVs and anecdotal evidence suggests that most of them end up in the shredding machine. The best way to strike up a relationship with a head-hunter is by getting an introduction. Find out if any of your colleagues and friends have ever been headhunted and, if so, get the head-hunter's name. Proceed from there by making contact on the phone. Send in your CV if you are asked to do so (suggest it, if necessary).

Summary

Being head-hunted attracts a premium and this is why cultivating head-hunters is a must for anyone with serious pay ambitions. Though being headhunted seems like an event over which you have no control, you can encourage it by:

- working on your Lifelong Interview skills
- extending your range of skills and broadening your experience
- paying attention to your networks (your circle of professional contacts)
- seeking to improve your visibility
- ensuring your visibility associates you with 'something good happening', e.g. a successful business outcome.

Having received an approach from a head-hunter you must milk the situation for all it's worth. Identify therefore situations in which:

- you have skills, experience, contacts or know-how which the head-hunter's client is anxious to acquire
- you are the only fish in the pond (or where you are one of very few), i.e. where alternatives to you are unavailable or in short supply.

Given these favourable circumstances you have formidable bargaining strength to your elbow and it is up to you to name your own price – bearing in mind that the biggest mistake you can make is to ask for too little. In all of this, view the head-hunter as someone who can:

- tip you off if your salary aspirations are beyond what the employer is prepared to pay
- do the soundings out for you
- help to forge the deal.

Verdict on being headhunted

Good points
An opportunity for making really big steps up the pay ladder.

Bad points
None!

10 | **WORKING FOR YOURSELF**

One way of getting better financial recognition for your talents is by forgoing the securities of employment and working for yourself. In this final chapter we are going to look at:

- Going it alone – what's in it for you
- The outsourcing option – taking some of the risk out of going solo by getting your employer to give you a start
- Making a success of working for yourself
- Ensuring the return and knowing when to call it quits

Is it for you?

Hitherto, a lot of the debate about working for yourself has centred around whether you're the right type or not. But with the changing patterns that modern careers follow, a twenty-first-century reality is that more and more people will work for themselves at some points in their lives. In other words:

- it's no longer such an oddball thing to want to do
- it's not confined to certain careers (e.g. journalism) – which tended to be the case in the past.

But is it for you? When it comes to looking at ways of making more money for yourself, is it an option you should be considering?

The answer lies in two parts:

1 From a purely practical point of view, is yours the kind of work you can do as a one-man/one-woman outfit or does it require team effort?

2 Is the opportunity there for you? Is there some way of going it alone and getting the rewards without incurring too many of the risks?

What's in it for you?

Before looking at these two considerations in more detail, let's address a more fundamental issue. What can you hope to get from working for yourself? What, in money terms, do you stand to gain?

In the short term, it probably boils down to the following:

■ quantity-wise, you can determine how much work you do – meaning, if you really do put in the effort, then the financial return will be there for you.

■ you can set your own price.

Note, however, that both of these items are market sensitive. In quantity terms, you won't get the work if the work isn't there. In price terms, you might find your customers asking you to make cuts when they're experiencing hard times. With your customers, remember, they're going to be bigger than you are. Equally, you could find you have a difficulty when you need to put your prices up from time to time.

⚠ WARNING!

Going it alone when the economy is about to go into recession is classic bad timing. So, if you're contemplating working for yourself, keep an eye on the economic indicators and, if they don't look good for any reason, put your decision on hold.

Further into the future, your decision to go it alone could lead to bigger and better things. Many very successful businesses started with someone somewhere deciding life would be better if they worked for themselves. Have dreams like this. It will do you good.

Assessing the risks

For many people contemplating working for themselves the biggest single obstacle in their minds is the risk they will be taking. But risk, as we have seen, always has two sides to it and, as with everything else to do with your career, it is important you look at both of them. Seen in this more balanced context, working for yourself can be more attractive than it sometimes seems at first sight. The upsides, in terms of opening up opportunities to line your pockets, look positively good, whereas the downsides, though not particularly pleasant, are little different to the downsides of making a bad job move. The message? Don't write off working for yourself simply because it looks dodgy. If (a) the conditions are right for you and (b) your aim is to get a better return for the effort you put in, then it could be a perfectly sensible option to go for. And, if the alternative happens to be staying put in some poorly paid, dead end job ... need we say more?

The outsourcing option

Is there anything you can do to minimize the downsides of going it alone?

Anyone who has worked for themselves will tell you, without a doubt, that the hardest part is at the beginning. You have no sales (no income) and in many cases this means possibly:

■ borrowing enough money to see you through your start-up period

■ digging into your savings.

There is a possibility, of course, that you could lose the lot, meaning that you won't just have the problem of rescuing your career – you could be left with a financial millstone round your neck as well. There are ways of guarding against failure but none are fail-safe. At this point let's bring in Georgia. The next case study describes her experiences at what seemed, first of all, like a black moment in her career.

CASE STUDY: GEORGIA

Georgia is a one-woman human resources department in a medium-sized manufacturing company which is part of a large group. Her responsibilities include recruitment, giving line managers guidance on how to deal with human resources problems and keeping the company updated on statutory requirements. She also doubles up as the company's Health and Safety Officer. Recently a new Group Chief Executive arrived on the scene and one of his first actions was to embark on a major restructuring exercise. The approach he took was as follows. He identified the core functions in each company in the group, then simply declared the rest surplus to requirements. Georgia thus saw her job swept away by someone she had only met briefly – a fact she found very hard to take in.

Two days after being given the bad news, Georgia went to see her boss, the Factory Manager. What's going to happen to all the jobs she does? she asked him. Who will do them after she's gone? The Factory Manager shrugged. He said the instruction from Head Office was to find outside suppliers for anything that couldn't be absorbed into other people's jobs. In the case of Georgia's work, because it's so specialized, the only viable option would seem to be to farm it out to a firm of Human Resources consultants at an enormous cost. Yes, it all seemed pretty crazy, the Factory Manager agreed. There again, most things coming out of Head Office these days seemed to be pretty crazy.

Reflecting on this conversation overnight, Georgia came up with a plan. Next day she went to see the Factory Manager again. How would it be viewed, she asked, if she set herself up as an independent human resources consultant and tendered for her own work? In terms of fees, she would charge exactly the same as the company currently pays for its human resources service, i.e. her salary plus the expenses of her office. In future and as part of the deal she would meet all her own expenses, of course.

When Georgia finished speaking, the Factory Manager's first question was to ask her if she was really serious. When she assured him that she was, he asked her for 24 hours to think through her proposal and discuss it with his senior management colleagues. They met again the following morning. The Factory Manager said he was more than happy to let Georgia carry on with the human resources work on an outsourced basis and that was also the consensus view among his colleagues. Apart from anything else, she knew the company and its requirements, and they knew her and the quality of her work. Neither would be the case, of course, with outside consultants. Would the Chief Executive have to give his approval to the idea? Georgia asked. The Factory Manager said no, adding that the Chief Executive was not the kind of person to want to get involved in too much detail.

Georgia's case study illustrates an interesting trend of recent years. In their urge to seek lean and minimalist solutions, more and more organizations are shedding functions they see as non-core and outsourcing them to external providers. The beneficiaries in many cases have been former employees and, from their point of view, having a secure source of income from day one of working for themselves prevents a financially precarious start-up period. The advantage for Georgia and others like her is that they can use this financial prop as a bouncing board to source other work. The income they get from this other work will then yield the gains that can be had from moving from employment to working for themselves.

Key points to pick out from this case study are as follows:

- As a one-woman department, the option of going solo was open to Georgia.
- The initial situation was a bad one as far as Georgia was concerned (imminent closure of her department). This demonstrates how outsourcing opportunities often come about from something that, on first appearances, seems 'bad'.

■ The Factory Manager and his colleagues were happy to proceed with Georgia because they knew her and the quality of her work, showing again the spin-offs to be had from practising good Lifelong Interview skills.

■ The idea to outsource the human resources came from Georgia herself. If she'd simply sat on her hands when she heard of her imminent redundancy, nothing would have happened (probably).

NOTEPAD

Given normal circumstances (i.e. not the kind of circumstances Georgia found herself in), outsourcing a function will probably be the furthest thought from an employer's mind. So, if this is a course you want to pursue you will probably have to sell the idea first. Why should they buy it? Again it comes back to your silent bargaining power. If they say no, they'll realize straight away that one of the consequences could be your decision to up and leave – in this case up and leave so you can go off and set up on your own. Given what may start to look to them like a stark choice, your employer will hopefully go for the least painful option for them, i.e. let you do your work on an outsourced basis.

Making a success of working for yourself

Bearing in mind you're doing this for the money, it goes without saying that you need to take full advantage of the opportunity that is now available to you. Principally, this means working at it but that isn't all. It also means being able to bring in work from other sources. This isn't so easy where your face isn't known and where, by definition, your Lifelong Interview skills can pull no strings for you. Where you can get work by recommendation (e.g. from your old firm or through your contacts) then so much the better but, where you have to resort to mailshots or cold canvassing to advertise what you have to offer, then it's only realistic not to set your expectations too high. In other words, it can be a long, hard slog before the benefits from building up a reputation as a good service provider start to trickle through to you.

But is there anything you can do in the meantime to get the money rolling in? One option is the contract or short-term assignment sector in which agencies or firms of consultants find the work for you. Who are these people? Again check out the business listings. Alternatively, keep your eye on the ads in the newspapers (agencies and firms of consultants often advertise for people to do fill-in jobs and short-term projects). You could also tap into your networks to see if anyone with similar skills to yours has ever had the experience of trying to find short-term work. Draw on any leads they can give you.

Key point

Making a success out of working for yourself (making money out of it) often means mixing 'n' matching, i.e. combining a hotch potch of different activities to make the end result add up. Don't hesitate to do this. In particular, don't see it as being beneath you. Working for yourself is a different ball game and the sooner you get used to the idea, the better it will be for you. See the variety as part of the fun.

When to call it quits

In terms of extending your skills and broadening your experience (adding value to yourself), working for yourself has much to commend it. And since adding value to yourself converts readily into silent bargaining power, the benefits carry forward into whatever you decide to do next.

This brings us to a fundamental point about doing a solo act for a while – there will probably come a time when it's sensible to call it quits.

CASE STUDY: VICKY

Vicky is a recruitment consultant who decided to work for herself 5 years ago when she saw the opportunities for making money. By and large she has done well – working from an office at home, hiring interviewing facilities when she needs to and servicing a small but loyal base of customers (people who know her and appreciate the good job that she does). Vicky's problem, however, is she's not sure where her career is going. If she worked in a large employment agency, she would be in a management position by now and earning a good salary.

Working for yourself means forgoing the promotion opportunities that would be available to you if you worked in a larger structure and the improved earnings that would go with it. In other words, working for yourself can lead to underachievement in earnings power in the longer term and the signs that this is happening are not always easy to pick up. The money still looks good and the realization that they're underachieving only occurs to some people who work for themselves when they see former colleagues (people who are still in regular employment) doing better than they are.

Key point

Unless you've got other reasons for wanting to go on working for yourself (like you've got designs on growing your one-person operation into a small business or you don't want to do anything else) be quite clear about where you see your exit points. In other words, when you've made the money, had the experience, proved whatever it was you wanted to prove to yourself, be prepared to leave it at that.

NOTEPAD

Working for yourself will be right for you at some point in your career – usually when the opportunity to do it on favourable terms presents itself.

Questions and answers

Outsourcing work to teams

Q *Like Georgia in your case study, my colleagues and I work in the Human Resources Department of a manufacturing company except, in our case, there are four of us who work together as a team. Coincidentally, there are rumours flying round that our work is about to be outsourced to a firm of consultants (a name has been mentioned). Whether this means we would be offered jobs with the consultants is not yet clear. Sensing, however, that we could be heading towards a precipice, my colleagues and I wondered whether to nip matters in the bud by putting in our own bid to run the Human Resources Department on an outsourced basis. Since the advice you give only relates to individuals operating on their own, what further points do we need to consider if we set out to do this as a team?*

A Once relationships with others come into play, it clearly gets a lot harder. Needless to say, your team will need some structure or corporate identity to it – meaning there are other matters to consider, such as shared ownership of assets and liability for debts. These are things that need setting out in a formalized legal agreement (get proper advice). Having said all this, there are some clear benefits to being a team, notably in terms of strength of numbers and the wider collective experience you will be able to draw on. A good place to start is by being honest with yourselves about how you get along together – bearing in mind that the road ahead is unlikely to be smooth. Assuming you will all have equal status in the new set-up (e.g. a formal business partnership), you will certainly need some method of ironing out disagreements. You could do this either by agreeing to go with the majority or by someone having a casting vote (a rotating chairman, perhaps). There is no reason why this shouldn't work out for you, but just be clear in your own minds that it will be very different to being employed.

Reverting back to employment after working for yourself

Q *From an employer's point of view, is there a stigma attached to people who have worked for themselves? In particular, will they be seen as people who will find it difficult to fit back in?*

A All employers are different and, yes, you will come across some who will view people who've worked for themselves as free-thinking, money-minded mavericks who will find it hard to settle back into the constraints of a normal job. Equally though, there will be others who will see people who have successfully gone it alone as courageous, self-disciplined and self-motivated, i.e. all good points. Bear in mind also that more and more people have worked independently at some point in their careers, so there is less tendency for it to be seen as an unusual thing to do. In other words, the kind of attitudes you're talking about are rapidly becoming part of the past.

Outsourcing at your employer's suggestion

Q *I am an IT specialist and the suggestion has recently been put to me to perform the function I carry out as an outside service provider rather than an employee. Understandably perhaps, I viewed this suggestion with suspicion at first then, the more I thought about it, the more I saw the possibilities. However, I still have some lingering concerns about loss of employment rights, security etc. – do you have any thoughts on how I should address these?*

A The fact that the suggestion to become an outside service provider has come from your employer clearly puts you in a much stronger position from the point of view of negotiating advantageous terms for yourself. They are obviously keen to see you take up this option hence they might be persuaded to be bountiful with arrangements to help you make the transition (and calm some of your fears). Possible areas to explore are as follows:

■ a cash lump sum (sufficient, say, to give you some working capital)

■ the gift of some of your equipment (or the option to purchase it on favourable terms)

■ a guarantee in the form of a contract that they will use your services for a fixed period e.g. two years.

Dangers of outsourced work

Q *Isn't there a danger with outsourced work that it will take up the lion's share of your available time meaning you won't be able to take on new clients?*

A Yes, there is a danger but it far outweighs the bigger danger of working for yourself and finding you don't have enough money coming in. In practice, there is usually some way of apportioning your time to ensure you don't fall into the trap of becoming a one-customer business and thus see no appreciable gains from going solo.

Summary

Stepping outside the normal framework of employment is not a route everyone would choose to follow, but it can provide opportunities for making a lot of money (more money than most people could hope to earn by doing the same thing in a normal job).

Without a doubt, the most difficult part of going it alone is at the beginning and this is why we have laid great emphasis in this chapter on the benefits of taking some of your old work with you into your new independent state. You can do this in two ways:

1 by jumping onto the outsourcing bandwagon (by getting your employer to let you carry on doing what you do now, but as an external supplier rather than an employee)

2 by keeping sweet with your former employer and thereby paving the way to ensuring they give you some work.

With the second of these points, the manner of your departure is obviously important. For instance, it won't do you any good at all if you use your handing in of your notice as an opportunity to get some longstanding grouses off your chest and/or tell the boss a few home truths!

If you secure a platform of steady work from your ex-employer, you can use this as a bouncing board to launch yourself onto a wider market. Here again your ex-employer will be useful to you. Some work you will only source by recommendation and, at this stage in your solo career, your ex-employer will be all that you have available to you. (Remember that your Lifelong Interview goes on working for you long after you have left an employer.)

Assuming you get over the hump of your start-up period and go on to make a success out of working for yourself, a question you need to keep asking is 'How long am I going to go on doing this for?' Unless you have entrepreneurial ambitions (to grow your one-man/one-woman act into something bigger), the gains from working for yourself tend to have a ceiling. There are only so many hours in the day, after all, and many independent service providers find it hard to escape from the hands-on work because there is no one else to delegate the routine tasks to. Once you have hit the ceiling (your maximum earnings capacity), you can only advance your earnings further by hiking up your prices (something market conditions may or may not allow you to do). The bottom line is this. If you want to go on climbing the pay ladder, you may – at some stage – need to move back into mainstream employment. The time spent working for yourself will have helped to broaden your outlook and experience – and hopefully you will have acquired a few more skills somewhere along the way too. In short, the working for yourself experience has added value to you and, in the fullness of time, this will benefit you in the shape of enhanced silent bargaining power.

Verdict on working for yourself

Good points

You could make a lot of money. Your income will come from more than one source. Working for yourself is self-selecting.

Bad points

The financial exposure during the start-up period can be considerable. This method of working takes you out of the mainstream. In the longer term, it can lead to underachievment.

GETTING A PAY RISE – A MODEL APPROACH

- See your best asset as yourself (always).
- Seek to add value to your best asset by extending your skills and broadening your experience.
- Polish up your image. Add even more value to yourself by practising your Lifelong Interview skills.
- Form an assessment of your silent bargaining power. What leverage can you can bring to bear on your employer? What would they gain by keeping you happy?
- Form an assessment of your employer's ability to deliver. Will the leverage work on them?
- Communicate your ambitions. Don't leave your employer in any doubt about what you want.
- Be aware when bargaining isn't working for you. Try to identify the reasons.
- Explore the possibilities for promotion. Will getting onto the next rung of the ladder open up the way to better pay for you?
- Think about whether relating some part of your pay to performance will help you. If the idea has merits, run it past your employer and see what reaction you get.
- Resort to the job market when you have to. Shop it intelligently. Don't let discouragement be the reason for giving up.
- View blackmail as a blunt-edged weapon. If you have to use it, be prepared for it to be messy.

■ Appreciate the premium attached to getting head-hunted. If you should be approached, don't squander the chance to make major leaps forward with your pay.

■ Include working for yourself among your options. Explore areas where it could advantage you and be on standby to spot any opportunities that might present themselves to do it on favourable terms.

INDEX

TEACH YOURSELF

WINNING AT JOB INERVIEWS
(Second edition)
Igor S. Popovitch

Teach Yourself Winning at Job Interviews shows you how to be the best applicant for the job you want.

Its clear, step-by-step format covers both basic and advanced strategies for winning in the job market, with example questions and model answers to help you:

- recognize and maximize your strengths
- present your weaknesses in a positive way
- evaluate interview situations and use them to your advantage
- deal with difficult or aggressive questions.

Igor S. Popovitch is the director of a career-help consultancy, offering training courses on interviewing, job hunting and career management.

NEGOTIATING

Phil Baguley

Teach Yourself Negotiating is an important book for all professionals. The need to negotiate effectively exists at all levels in all organizations. Whether you are dealing with colleagues, suppliers or customers you need to be able to negotiate – and do it well.

A book you cannot afford to be without, *Teach Yourself Negotiating*:

- shows you how to prepare for, carry out and complete your negotiations
- helps you decide what strategies and tactics to use
- illustrates how to use the bargaining process to generate a successful outcome
- guides you to a successful implementation of that outcome
- provides a checklist for assessing your own negotiating skills.

Phil Baguley is an experienced business writer and lecturer. He has held senior management roles in multinational corporations and has also worked as a management consultant in the UK and Europe. He is also the author of *Teach Yourself Project Management*.

Other related titles

TEACH YOURSELF

WINNING IN THE JOB MARKET

Mark Hempshell

Teach Yourself Winning in the Job Market is a comprehensive guide to getting ahead in today's competitive climate. It shows you how to find the job or career that is right for you, whether part or full time, at home or abroad, and provides a detailed 'action plan' to help you get a more rewarding and better paid job.

The book gives:

- a helping hand for everyone in today's job market including young people, students and those already in – or out of – work
- clear, practical, step-by-step advice that you can really use
- clever hints and tips that will give you the competitive edge and help you get the job you really want!

Mark Hempshell is an expert on job-hunting. He has written a number of books on the subject and is the editor of *International Job Finder* magazine.

TEACH YOURSELF

PERFORMANCE APPRAISALS

Polly Bird

All managers have to carry out staff appraisals, and *Teach Yourself Performance Appraisals* provides the guidelines and help on how to do this effectively and obtain the desired results. The book deals with each stage of appraising, from preparation to evaluation. It also gives advice on how to cope with difficulties during the appraisal process, as well as how to handle your own appraisal.

The book is written in a practical and straightforward way and includes:

- guidance to managers new to appraisals, and those who want to improve
- advice on how to turn discussion into action
- help with upward appraisals.

Polly Bird is a professional writer of business and training books.

Other related titles

BUSINESS PRESENTATIONS

Angela Murray

Giving a presentation can be a daunting and nerve-racking experience, even for a regular presenter – what can you do to give yourself confidence and ensure success? *Teach Yourself Business Presentations* provides the answer. From defining the brief to post-presentation analysis, the book supplies a step-by-step guide to the skills and techniques needed to deliver an effective, engaging presentation.

Team presentations, presentatons to colleagues, informative and persuasive presentations – appropriate techniques are considered for these and many more. Throughout the book imagination, innovation and creativity are all actively encouraged.

Covered in the book:
■ strategic planning – defining and analysing a brief
■ planning and research
■ creativity
■ communication skills
■ audio-visual aids
■ 'presentation etiquette' and personal presentation
■ analysing performance.

An easy-to-read guide, full of hints and tips, this book provides support and guidance for the novice, and fresh ideas for the more experienced.

Angela Murray is a freelance Business Consultant in marketing communications and presentation skills.